Ageless Living
_____

Freedom From The Culture of Death

Mony Vital, Ph.D.

Ageless Living, Freedom from the Culture of Death
Copyright © 2005 by Mony Vital
Del Mar, CA

ISBN: 0-966010-41-8

Library of Congress Catalogue Card Number: 9790767

Book cover, graphic designs & editing:
Stephanie Heinze, Creative Director
Creative Shark Marketing & Design, Carlsbad, CA
www.creativeshark.com

Publisher: Vital Publishing, Del Mar, CA

All Rights Reserved
No part of this work may be reproduced, stored in a retrieval system, or transmitted by any means; electronic, mechanical, photocopying, recording or otherwise, without prior written permission from the author: Mony Vital 1-888- 225-7501

Acknowledgments

I have been blessed with and would like to thank a growing circle of great humans who kept urging me to publish this material so they can have it for themselves to work on and expand their own transformation.

To my colleague Audre'D. DeNard for sharing her research on choices in this work.

To Jasmuheen, the mother of "Living on Light", for bringing to the world her high passion for transforming humanity into it's unlimited possibility.

I would also like to than Kevin Trudeau for this contribution to the world with his timely and valuable book *Natural Cures "They" Don't Want You to Know About*. Thanks to Jean-Claude Koven for bringing a deeper dimension to the exploration of inner-realities. And to my dear friend Margot Anand, who is a source of inspiration, bringing her vitality into her work with Tantra and transformation.

My deep personal and sincere appreciation to Kimberly Wagner for editing the manuscript. Her editorial skills and her knowledge and understanding of the subject of physical immortality truly enhance the clarity of my message.

Disclaimer

This book is designed to provide information in regard to the subject matter covered only. It is sold with the understanding that the publisher and author are not engaged in rendering any form of therapy, counseling, medical treatment or diagnosis. If you think you have a medical problem, please see your doctor or dial 911.

Acknowledgements

Ageless Living and the information in it will complement and supplement other texts and other ideas. You are urged to read all the available material, learn as much as possible about managing your mind, body, spirit and energy, and tailor the information to your individual needs.

The primary purpose of this manual is to educate and enlighten. The author and Vital Publishing shall have neither liability nor responsibility to any person or entity with respect to any loss, damage caused, or alleged to be caused, directly or indirectly, by the information contained in this book. Therefore, this text should be used only as a general guide for cosmic development.

How To Read This Book

There is something for everybody in *Ageless Living*. The writing style is a reflection of the author's lectures, speaking engagements, seminars and workshops. It is expressed in the speaking style of a foreigner residing in the U.S.

- Reading the first few chapters for the first time may cause the following reactions: anger, fear, uncertainty, loss, annoyance, upset, regret, frustration, powerlessness, dreaming, visualizing, relief or understanding. Continue to read, don't stop. It's not the writing; it's your stuff coming up to face you.
- *Ageless Living* is best understood when read very slowly. (It's not a novel.)
- Read *Ageless Living* regularly and often; make it your personal encyclopedia for how to evolve and become an ageless physical being.
- If you're susceptible to new ideas, continue reading this guide at your own risk.

Preface

I am elated to convey more understanding and clarity on the subject of longevity and what physical immortality really means. Every human being has the notion that he or she may be able to live forever, live longer, experience optimal well-being, or become an ageless physical being at some point in their life. This book *Ageless Living* is a replacement for my earlier book, *Life Unlimited*. I wanted to create a more precise and direct exploration of physical immortality, to alleviate any confusion as to what it means and to add more of my personal experiences.

All the basic beliefs and principles which I laid out ten years ago, remain accurate, precise and to the point according to my approach to life.

In the years since the publication of *Life Unlimited*, I have examined and re-examined my thinking, understanding, behavior and perspective regarding the choice of living as an ageless being. I find my path to be very inspiring, fulfilling and rewarding as I experience a high level of well-being and total love for ecstatic living. In this book I will share with you personal developmental information, and stories of events which have shaped my understanding and my point of view in life. There will be new chapters on energetic balancing, breatharianism and dark room workshops.

Throughout the book, I mention a process I call "living as physically immortal (LAPI)". My intention is to produce a conceptual framework and guidelines for using LAPI throughout life, and a set of markers that help to evaluate progress at all times. The goal is to strip from physical immortality the shroud of secrecy and confusion that most of you may have encountered already in your effort to learn more or to become "alive" physical beings.

Most (with a few exceptions) of the writings from other authors on personal transformation and spiritual enlightenment of the last few decades reflect that all of the writers personally and communally did not believe in their physical bodies. They discarded and discredited the physical option for longevity in favor of the spiritual one. This fragmentation of the being is the center point of our cultural beliefs as they stand now, and has been continually inserted deeper in us, as if we humans, smilingly have no other options. This trend in writing is the reflection of our culture's powerless ability to cope with death issues and see their true implications. For that reason, a great section of the population is at physical and mental unease, confused and demoralized about the answers they are getting, and about the results in their lives.

In reference to my writing style, I speak directly to the reader in a way that leaves no doubt about my intention to convey an uncompromised position and not to delete the energy and dynamics of the conceptual programs. I do not claim to have all the answers, or to imply that my way of approaching life is the only way for everyone else. Absolutely not. Some individuals will be helped in improving their lives and well-being, even if they practice in just a limited fashion.

In regard to gender references throughout the book, I have tried to use the pronouns he/she, his/her, etc., equally and would like to emphasize that I am addressing the collective in equality in the majority of instances.

Ageless living represents a life stand, a vision, an outcome, and a reality. Every time I say or think the words ageless living, a symbol or signature of well-being is displayed, causing a fresh flow of warm energy to run all over my body. For me, ageless living is an ecstatic urge that turns me on. It is fun, very creative, has no limits, has no obstructions it is living your art, and is the best improvisation situation you'll ever play or experience.

In my world, the choices are simple, my path is clear, my destiny is carved and I am the designer of it. Living as an "alive" being is the most rewarding interior design project I have taken on. Ageless living is the response to high life force (chi). When energy flows unimpeded in the body, as the rule, you are living as an ageless being. Letting my mind journey into uncharted worlds of unlimited possibilities and choosing life as the only imprint I have, is my natural state.

My goal in writing this book is to reach other human beings who want to change and create a different way of living. And to those like myself, who felt profoundly different from their siblings in their youth, who still feel different from their friends and counterparts in adulthood, and who have had little or no validation for their unique approach to life. I hope to reach other individuals who function on a "life instinct," that is, staying truly alive on the fringes of the framework and context of this society, but not part of it. Those who courageously maintain sovereignty on the edges of the acceptable myths and beliefs that exist in today's culture and to say "Hello!"

Table of Contents

Chapter 1: Introduction 17

Chapter 2: Concepts of Mortality
A view of mortality 21
Mortality journey 26
Medicine & illness 28
Origins of illness 30
Beliefs & biology 31
Confusion 37

Chapter 3: Culture of Death Benefactors
Desanctifying religion 39
Social & governmental influence 43
The critical nature of choice 47
Pretending 50

Chapter 4: An Exploration of Physical Immortality
Introduction 53
A view of limmortality 56
No limitation 58
Body cues 61
Role playing 62

Chapter 5: Advantages of Physical Immortality
Wholeness 65
Body-mind unity 66

xii Table of Contents

Control over the immune system 68

Eliminating pain & disease 71

Age cessation 73

No more fear 74

Joy, fun & vitality 75

Participation in life 75

Fulfillment in life 76

Purpose & essence of life 78

Higher spirituality 78

Chapter 6: Considerations for Physical Immortality

Introduction 83

47 questions to ponder 85

Choice 89

Awareness for creation 90

Chapter 7: The Path to Immortality

The Element of wishing 93

Readiness for truly living 94

The dying guru 95

Placement of beliefs 96

A gentle look at the process 97

Groundwork for LAPI 98

The new experiene 100

Chapter 8: Beginning Your Journey

Introduction 103

Immortality in this society 105

                    Lists for improvement 106

                    Trauma clearing 109

                    Forgiveness 112

                    Deprogramming 112

                    Programming power 115

                    A story—my early days 117

Chapter 9:   **Methods & Practices**

                    Self-healing 121

                    The breath 122

                    Posture, entergy & what it reveals 124

                    Exercise 127

                    Age reversal 129

                    Yoga 131

Chapter 10: **Moving into LAPI**

                    Markers of physical immortality 133

                    More LAPI advantages 138

                    Starting—the commitment 139

                    Creating new worlds 143

                    Persistency 147

Chapter 11: **Body Detoxification**

                    Cellular communication 151

                    Power of influence 152

                    Body cleansing & purification 152

                    Parasite contamination 153

                    Information for parasite cleanses 155

                    Importance of pH balance 157

Table of Contents

    Acid forming foods 158
    Alkaline forming foods 159

Chapter 12: Living on Light & Nutrition
    In the beginning 161
    Nutrition & well-being 162
    Body wonder 163
    Breatharianism & living on light 165
    Living on light—my personal experience 168

Chapter 13: The Joy of Relationships
    Got intimacy? 173
    Intimacy & sex 174

Chapter 14: On the Path
    Love without limitation 181
    Volunteering your life 182
    Selfishness & selfullnes 186
    Present history 188
    Others on the path 189
    Changing frequency 190
    The body electric 191
    Energetic connection 192
    The bird people 195

Chapter 15: Energetic Balancing
    Frequency of prayer 199
    Laws of creation—basic information—

quantum world 199
The Quantum Prayer System for energetic
balancing 201
Healing prayer=symbols=energy 203
Detoxification 205
Things you need to know about the
Quantum Prayer System 206

Chapter 16: The Dark Room
Dark room advantages 209
My dark room experience 210
The monitors of the dark room 212

Chapter 17: Cosmic Connection
Being in this world 215
Ascension 217
Participating in the world 218
Transformation 219
Names for the living 220
The creator 222
Conclusion 223

Appendix: Contact Information 227

The Purpose of Life Extension

Becoming a complete human

Living in optimal health

Finding wholeness & oneness

Loving & cherishing your physical being

Ending the personal suffering & pain of dying

Choosing to live the life you want, after you truly get to know yourself

Making a positive difference in the lives of others

Forming a special relationship with the creator

Figure 1: Life Extension

Chapter 1

Introduction

Ageless living is the outcome of a different lifestyle than the one you are familiar with. This lifestyle is based on the practices of living as physically immortal. The central emphasis in this exploration is upon the physical body—it is the most valuable gift that anyone will ever have and enjoy. Most people spend more money, time and muster more effort to clean their clothes, than in caring for their body and mind. If you are interested in living a life without limitation, and want to experience the feeling of being truly alive, then this work may give you the knowledge to experience it. It can bring you closer to your ideal state, and your intrinsic, original thoughts.

The ideas of physical immortality provide a unifying focus from which to comprehend and appreciate your physical body, your feelings, and your emotions. Maybe you have already been working toward physical immortality in this, and/or, several previous lifetimes. Perhaps this lifetime is the charm for you and it is going to happen in a real, easy and loving way.

I am writing this book to reaffirm the principles and beliefs that I feel strongly about—living as an "alive" being, in spite of being surrounded by the trappings of the culture of death that we all live in. This book examines physical immortality in such a manner as to make the possibility of actual longevity a very reasonable and sensible goal. It provides a model by which individuals may integrate the ideal of physical immortality, even within the individual's limitations, their present circumstances and biological profile—in a way which will enable them to move beyond limiting conditions into another paradigm. To reclaim their fullest and most authentic lives, where true aliveness is fostered.

18   Ageless Living, Freedom From The Culture of Death

Both general and specific dynamics of the historical aspects of social, cultural and economic constraints that are placed in opposition to the idea of an ageless society will be identified and examined. These issues include aspects related to the physical well-being of the human body, as well as the emotional and spiritual aspects, identified as social norms, that may shorten or lengthen the lifespan of the individual. Secondary areas of focus include the physical body as a receiver to its environment, (i.e., one who is not yet in control of the forces which influence him), body-mind unity, and disease control.

The words "physical immortality" are the only available and suitable words in the English language that describe life beyond its standard meaning, presently portrayed in this culture. These words are simple and communicate to the subconscious. The words "physical immortality" reflect longevity, optimal health, physical longevity, living forever, life without limitation and unlimited life span.

I will address a number of questions seeking answers in this book, such as the following:

- What is the concept of physical mortality?
- What social, economic, and cultural factors tend to influence the concept of physical mortality?
- What physical, psychological and emotional factors can be identified that influence physical mortality and the average life-span in humans?
- How do beliefs influence the biological health of the human body in relation to the concept of physical immortality?
- What is spirituality and how does it influence mortality and longevity?
- If we are energetic beings, how does energy conduct our lives?
- What is nourishment? Is pranic nourishment real?
- How can one integrate and experience physical immortality?

Chapter 1: Introduction

Several topics related to physical mortality and physical immortality are discussed and examined with a review in the area of human longevity and the works of others on the subject of immortality.

Later discussion presents specific methods and practices that one may utilize as one enters the process of living as a physically immortal person. The importance of breathwork, exercise and nutrition are discussed and offered as practical ways to participate in life enhancement for optimum health. The process of living as physically immortal (LAPI) will be examined, providing markers and progress indicators to help beginners address their individual needs and personal hindrances.

As you enter the process of physical immortality, spiritual enlightenment is a natural outcome. Here I am speaking of spiritual enlightenment in its actual and purest form. Closeness to your God-Creator is a matter of fact. Accessing a direct line of communication with your God-Creator becomes a very simple task when you are living as an ageless being. You do not need a middle man or clergy to facilitate contact and communication with your Creator.

The work I present here is timely. This exploration offers an approach toward a new concept of physical mortality and another choice for individuals to make, to live as ageless beings. It is also my intention to present a rationale and methodology for the possibility of living one's life as physically immortal—essentially a therapeutic model for longevity. Traditional interpretation of "healthy living" and the aging process has shifted, where new opportunities and demands require individuals to independently think and redefine what they experience as "living" in all aspects and dimensions of their existence.

The life force and vitality level of an individual, which is influenced by many factors, is the originator of his or her longevity, the singular, most substantive and irreplaceable force to maintain life on any and all levels.

20   Ageless Living, Freedom From The Culture of Death

In spite of the work of Deepak Chopra and others who suggest an alternative to mortality, western society depicts, regulates and determines what is to be the average life span of a human being. We give these implications and standards power and authority as a result of their societal origins—the governing bodies and "experts in the field".

Who dares to question the statistics and actuarial tables presented annually by the nation's insurance organizations? If the tables tell you that you have 12 years left to live, 20 years, or 30 years, you generally accept it to be a given. It is only truth in the sense that the information is accepted by your mind and cells of your body, and that you won't question the validity of the information—which may be false and a form of soft mind control perpetrated by the culture. Your mind and body accept and believe it to be true through your acceptance, without verifying its authenticity. Most have not been given an alternative to this reality.

Furthermore, by surrendering to this dictate you are operating on a default mode and limiting your choices and options. The presence or absence of the individual's personal responsibility will determine the lifestyle choices for establishing personal regimens in keeping with physical well-being.

Essentially, in this book I share my life experience with you, and offer you the knowledge that I have come to find in my life as a practicing physically immortal human being. It is my hope that by doing so, my work may touch you in such a way as to raise your body vibration a few notches higher as you continue to build upon that level, bringing you to a state of oneness and unity with all the parts that are "you".

Chapter 2

Concepts of Mortality

A view of mortality
One major objective of this writing is to help individuals recognize their own abilities and reach a vision of themselves and their surroundings from a higher point than society dictates for them. The greater and more broad the point where one's perspective originates, the greater the vision one holds. This is truly a precondition for awareness and transformation.

No matter what life experiences you hold, the view of the culture of death which I will present here may cause you to think more critically about your way of life and, little by little, get acquainted with your belief system. This awareness will open new possibilities for more life-enhancing beliefs. Your sincerity and commitment to the dignity of the physical body, as well as the psychological and social aspects of yourself, will never be the same again.

There is no neutral stand for you to take—your instinctive urges, thoughts and senses will be activated and surface to the forefront. Your mind and ego will play a big role in the way you will process the information. Inner role-playing will bring out the victim and the persecutor aspects at once—at the same time. Perhaps a frightening journey at first, if you stay on this inner journey long enough, it just may become fun—surely, it will be a departure from the mundane, boring future-less life that you and the world have offered yourself so far!

The belief in death of the physical body is ingrained in the psyche from very early childhood when those beliefs were first installed by the parents of the child. Other adult figures confirmed the message, and as the child grew, his or her peers validated the idea of the certainty of death as an inevitable outcome. Thus, the death belief is one of the most easily accepted without question.

In our culture the presence of death in every person's life experience is a learned occurrence. Death has become a regular, normal and expected outcome and is recognized and accepted in all societies. In addition to this, all religious beliefs are based on, and foster the death belief.

In today's society, death is the common denominator upon which national and international governments base their population statistics. Death and death statistics have been, and continue to be used as the basis for social and civil appropriations and in the planning of future development. All modern and modernizing countries use mortality tables as statistical markers in their planning. In a modern society, no activity related to men, women, or children's daily living escapes the influence and interpretation of social planning using mortality rates, authorized to govern the citizens of a nation. From this observation, the inference can be made that there is little, if any, escape from the social acceptance of death, and this further deepens the belief.

Looking at Figure 2, you will notice a graph that indicates the currently accepted lifespan. At one end is a mark of the date of birth, and at the other end is a mark of the date of death. This is the length of life any person can expect to live. This illustration depicts and describes the cycle of life as we know it. Look at the process by which a young boy or girl begins to become acquainted with the idea of death, and starts to accept death as a fact of reality. This process starts very early in life, as the child usually first learns of the concept of death when overhearing his/her parents and other adults in their conversations. The child also learns in his earliest school years from his teachers that there is an end to life, and this end is called death. Then, when that child goes to church, he is introduced to the concept of death, now as a requisite for salvation and an end to the harshness of life. He will learn that he is here on Earth only temporarily, and his most purposeful life goals, his real life, will start later (heaven). Thus, the child now totally believes in death, and knows that he will definitely die at some point in time in the future.

Chapter 2: Concepts of Mortality

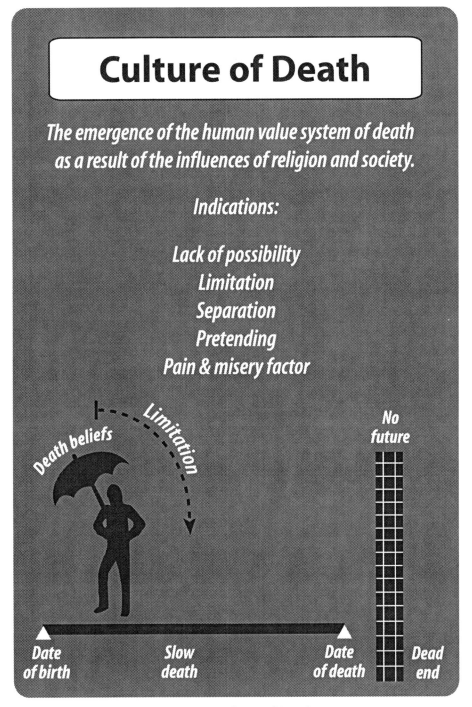

Figure 2: Culture of Death

At this critical point in the child's life, he or she will contemplate this in an attempt to make sense out of the new belief. However, with the limitations of childhood and only the earliest stages of emotional and psychological development in the youngster, he has tremendous obstacles to truly comprehending the concept of death. Essentially, what the child takes from this overheard information is that there is a real possibility that he or she may become an orphan. This event is very disturbing and forms the basis of all other subsequent occasions where the topic of death is introduced. Throughout the rest of childhood, the boy or girl usually receives affirmative connotations (death relieves suffering, death allows you to enter heaven, etc.) regarding the death that will surely come, mostly from teachers and religious clergy—those professing to be God's representatives. The belief becomes slowly and absolutely ingrained. The belief goes deep into the subconscious, sinking into the bottom of the "container", and then becomes the foundation upon which all other related beliefs are given final definition.

When the child reaches adulthood, he is already saturated with the numerous messages of death received from many directions—parents, culture, television, radio—society refers to death not by name or specific definition anymore, but as a passive certainty, implied in much of what he sees around him. Most of the messages are subliminal in nature, in the sense that they are subconsciously conveyed, and we accept them without any question or ability to filter out the hidden affirmation of death that is buried inside the message.

At this point, the adult knows that he or she must die. What occurs next is the construction of a subconscious expectation delegating the amount of time he/she allows for their life. The question is: how long should I live? Most individuals use the method of imitation to estimate the length of their lives, comparing and estimating the longevity within their own family and peers. From this, they decipher what their lifespan is to be.

Once the decision has been made, the body will start adjusting itself to a long-range death plan. The subconscious now has permission to direct or influence the bodily systems so that the desired goal is facilitated. The outcome will match the decision. These decisions are made at different levels of consciousness, and this type of resolution is a subliminal one. The resolution to die, the thoughts formed by this resolution, and the wording of the wish are very important elements. Occasionally the exact words will come out during different processes (i.e.; counseling) to clear trauma or stress-related illnesses. The installed belief systems become distilled and are represented through other drives, such as maladaptive sexual urges or the neurotic use of food, both of which originate in instinctive functions. Interestingly, these instinctual inner drives, since they are fundamental to all, also become very effective means of controlling the psychophysiology of the masses.

The expectation (and the intensity of it), for the length of one's lifespan relates directly to the beliefs in death and effects the degree to which the body promotes the breakdown of the immune system's ability to protect itself. Consequently different types of illnesses will follow. Some of these illnesses may be associated with a subconscious choice or merely acquired by way of imitation of others. This kind of resolution-generated activity is very common in all age groups. Ignoring and dismissing the emotional symptoms, fearing professional help when under stress, and isolation when in severe personal difficulty causes the individual to turn inward to get answers. In this space and mindset, the individual works with the only options he or she has available personally. In most cases, these options are limited, more or less, to the primitive interpretations of a child's point of view. This "childish" point of view is an incomplete picture of what life represents. This point of view is comprised of juvenile judgments, uncertainty, and a disjointed assembly of spurious remembrances of the environment. It is little more than an escape to a deeper void.

To undo a death wish or negative experience by trying to forget the event is only a superficial act. This action and thinking has no real meaningful application toward "undoing" the negativity of the event. In fact, the negative communication of forgetfulness is only superficial at best—the memory of the event has been buried deeper inside the body.

It is the same with the concept of death. Simply wishing it to go away never works. Thinking that we can forget our death wishes and urges simply by storing the memories of these events in a different or hidden location is nothing more than deleting the shortcut to the memory of the event. It is a form of denial and pretending.

Mortality journey
When a young adult reaches the point where he feels a need to form some definitive plans for his life and his future, he needs to make sense of how and why those external influences direct him to think that he has only a very small window of possibility for creating his life. The young adult looks ahead into the future, and realizes that he has only a limited future and a limited time to live and experience living. As absurd as it may seem, the young adult, while generating youthful plans and directions for his life, is in actuality already declining and preparing for his death. Given this scenario, he believes that he is given no choice, and most of his decline is being processed and performed by the subconscious. It is almost as if there are two different entities in one body, both ignoring the other. There is no possibility for this individual to see beyond the "death vision", depicted in the illustration as an open umbrella carried above his head at all times. This umbrella is marked "death" in large letters to remind him not to look any further, to remind him not to look beyond the space allowed below the umbrella.

As you can see from Figure 2, if there is no long-term future charted, envisioned or recognized, beyond the culture's time line, there is no possibility for a long-distance view of life and living.

Logically, the older and further into adulthood the individual gets, the greater the desperation and apathy felt. As he begins to see less and less of a future for himself, and feels his time is limited, a painful urgency usually ensues. This urgency may be manifested in bursts of irrational behaviors over the years, or in a slow ebbing away of spirit and connection with all that is alive around him. If he feels that he has heretofore lived a life without meaning and outcome, and he feels that little, if any time will be available to him to reconcile these issues, then his pain is surely monumental. Sometimes individuals who recognize that death is imminent may evince a tendency to pretend that everything is okay. An attempt to detach from the painful reality occurs, and wishing for forgetfulness to pacify his mind activity is undertaken. Thus, as the old sayings go, "time heals all wounds" or "things aren't so bad"—phrases used to facilitate a forgetting program to help deal with the prospect of death.

Pretending games, of course, are played at different levels throughout a person's life. An individual plays how much better he is than his neighbors and friends, how much more successful he is in comparison to his colleagues. For the pretender, the acquisition of material items is helpful—they are tangible and they bring a sense of success. This helps the psyche—the personal vision is allowed to become clouded in order not to see the pain, emptiness and the diaspora.

While traveling along the path in Figure 2, what is ever apparent is that life is declining from adulthood to the date of death. During the declining period, the individual is aware of and believes the end of his life is ahead, and this is generally acceptable to him. This awareness is quiet and private. Most people will not raise the subject in public, and very seldom is there a discussion even in a private setting. Most of the inquiries are introspective in nature—the person makes a silent journey in his inner thoughts and asks questions to himself only. Sometimes these issues will come up during a regression session, after a major life event or a realization/retrieval of memories from the subconscious.

The cultural belief system in the acceptance of death is so rooted that even the idea of not dying sounds unreal, unwarranted, and is a total denial. And many will say "Who needs it?" or "That's not possible", that is, to live a prolonged life. It is a true feeling for them, they have so completely accepted the belief in death and their lives have often become dismal. They feel there is nothing that they can do about it. These men and women are dying, slowly but surely, they are enveloped in a hopeless feeling that empties the vitality from the body.

To be sure, to watch the body die slowly is very depressing—everything biologically important is becoming out of control. Depression is rampant, and many men and women commit suicide from the lack of future and lack of possibility. The act of committing suicide is also, in part, an extension of living in denial or the extension of pretense when it becomes an unbearable game to continue playing. Actually, the reason for committing suicide seems reasonable. Shortening the time of unbearable pain is a more practical solution. Therefore, it seems that an individual considering suicide is looking to shorten his misery and suffering.

Out of control feelings manifest many different things at many different levels, including:

- the acceptance of the current and present status quo;
- the body following your thoughts, "then doing its own thing"—it becomes out of control;
- dominance of negative thoughts;
- the realization of wasting a life—having no purpose;
- knowing the truth about yourself, not knowing how to enact changes, or even that it is a possibility;
- the inner child in panic;
- the world shrinking inward;
- panic conditions; and
- wanting to die.

In all of this, an overwhelming sense of helplessness is very common, and all the fairy dreams in the world cannot deter the aging process.

Medicine & illness
Most sick people will tell you that they don't have a clue as to why they are sick—in fact, they will say it is out of character for them to be sick and they simply hate their disease. This causes an even deeper denial because now they must deal with the factor and denial of blame. This is a position of victimhood that further establishes and enables the disease.

As long as denial is in a prominent position, no real progress is going to occur. The inevitable disappointment regarding their inability to improve their physical condition comes as a tough awakening to them. For the unaware and indoctrinated person, there is no apparent means available by which they can affect the outcome of their disease, much less change the direction toward a positive outcome and renewed health. Medical treatment, as we know it, can assist a sick individual only on a symptomatic basis and only by treating obvious localized conditions. No doctor by himself or herself can cause the patient to be healed.

It is the patient's job to heal him or herself from the inside out. The patient must take charge of his own life, knowing that he was the one who produced the disease from the beginning! Therefore, it is only the patient who can undo his or her illness. To be sure, the traditional medical professional does a marvelous job of treating physical symptoms and alleviating pain, and this truly helps some reach a level of comfort. However, the medical establishment does not address the real issue at hand, namely to find the primary cause that originated and is the reason for the illness.

Here it is important to always keep in mind that humans are composed of an integration of three components that together make up a functional being: the mind, spirit, and the physical body which is energetic. All three are inextricably connected or merged, and all three are solidified as one harmonious system, with all memory from the day of birth stored and present inside the physical body. There are only a few doctors who ascribe to this analysis in dealing with the causes rather than the symptoms of disease. Nonetheless, these few are working with their patients in regard to changing the basic life patterns with amazing success (Simonton 1992). In doing so, they are revitalizing and reversing some of the so deeply buried and scrupulously hidden death wishes of their patients. This is a great beginning, yet with still a long way to go.

30   Ageless Living, Freedom From The Culture of Death

The standard representation of the death process as described, is a depiction where most individuals may have already given up on life and living, in their earliest days of childhood. However, in the realm of immortality, individuals can be reassured that whatever wishes and new inspirations and desires they have, they can indeed be made to manifest and come alive, despite the negative cultural influence on their spirit, soul and body. The imprinting and indoctrination of the death beliefs of culture and society are not inviolable. Those death beliefs can be deleted. No human being is unilaterally and forever obliged to believe in and conform to one or any aspect of a society or culture—free will makes that so. All humans, without exception, will continue to have the issue of death surface in their lifetimes, frequently enough to keep the mind engaged with the subject. (The issue often surfaces on birthdays and special anniversaries.) As a result, confusion and depression are very common occurrences in this culture.

Origins of illness

Where does disease come from? Well, in order for a disease to manifest, there are a few things that need to happen prior to the onset. The first is a belief system which promotes the death of the body. Inherently, when an individual assimilates the death belief, this in turn redirects the immune system in such a way that it alters its path to accommodate the death belief, and, unfortunately to fulfill the desired and seemingly unsolicited negative outcome.

With children who manifest illness and disease, the argument is—how does a child understand and accept the death belief at that age? Unequivocally, babies carry the energetic frequencies of the parents, beginning at the moment of conception. Because we are energetic beings, who resonate with frequencies of the surrounding "matrix", we naturally imitate, accept and adopt these resonant frequencies. In 99% of all children who have dysfunction around the time of birth and thereafter, the parent's death urges were resonating the highest and were evoked at the time of pregnancy. The argument that children cannot possibly know about death is totally baseless. It is the culture's inability to consider the fact that the body is energetically tuned, and constantly harmonizes its frequency of operation with the outside matrix.

Truly, it is the ability of the body-mind to create or undo any dysfunction through the internal messages that the subconscious receives, which makes the human body the marvel that it is. As you are realizing so far, the only way to acquire a disease is to create it from thoughts and beliefs, by imitating the frequencies of the disease, or by the dysfunctional information from others in your close environment. In our culture, it has unfortunately become a practice to promote and advertise diseases and syndromes for the sake of supposedly creating awareness of the disease, or for the prevention of and "fight against" it. However, the opposite is the outcome.

The more people identify with the dysfunction and accept it, the more their body will resonate with the imbalanced frequency of the advertised and declared disease. They then become susceptible to promoting and creating the disease in their own body—a good example is breast cancer. The more it is promoted, the more women participate in the culture's ideas and receive the toxic information about the disease, then more of them will be prone to the symptoms and developing it. It is easy to point to all kinds of theories, whether genetic or environmental. In my opinion, this is a form of cop-out response from the FDA and denial in individuals, when no other means of resolution is found to explain the reason for this major out break in cancer. Cancer finds it roots in the emotional makeup of the individual and healing occurs when the toxic information behind the symptoms is addressed, whether the person does this consciously or not.

Beliefs & biology
Belief systems are the first of the three instigators of functions that the body must engage to stay alive. Beliefs are the blueprint and the controller of our DNA programming. Until now our culture and the medical world have been searching in total darkness, working with an incorrect basic assumption about the body's code, thinking it is permanently

stored in the DNA. and therefore, needs to be tweaked to create changes in the body operation. The whole genome code and research conversation is a twist away from the real biology of the body which is our beliefs. The DNA function is a reflection of and is only good as operated and altered by one's beliefs which motivate it to construct specific actions.

The second function is our breath—breathing is an art of life. The quality and speed of breathing will determine the life span of the individual. Breathing is not only an autonomic function which has an on/off switch, instead breath has advanced settings which are chosen and learned options.

The third function relates to energy flows found in the body—a life force level and vitality (chi), and the level of harmony exhibited by these flows within the depths and surfaces of the physical layers. The body will always follow up on the beliefs, resolutions, commitments, wishes and instincts that the person has made, either consciously or unconsciously, by way of direct or indirect interjection of these beliefs and myths that the individual accepts and abides by.

Once the connection between beliefs and well-being become apparent, any change in one's belief system causes the body to react differently on all levels of function. For example, changing the belief system that a change in weather automatically causes you to have a headache, a runny nose and respiratory symptoms. This is a very common belief that is based on an utter and complete misconception of a myth. Once the individual accepts that particular belief, the physical symptoms will appear accordingly. Removing the belief, will result in dramatic changes in the condition of the individual. Once one realizes that the power of belief can indeed alter physical function and reality, thus the genetic make-up of the human cell, it is easier to understand that many, if not all beliefs are programs from the past, baseless, and may equally be changed for life giving beliefs that promote a positive outcome.

Chapter 2: Concepts of Mortality 33

Stress

Pathology of Stress

Stress accumulation
Stess compounding
Stress revolt
Surrender to stress
Giving up
Despair
Death wish
Illness & disease
Accelerated aging
Deterioration

The stress factor is the leading cause of death
(and the primary source of the inception of most illness)

Dr. Holmes & Dr. Fahe Social Readjustment Rating Scale

Figure 3: Stress

34   Ageless Living, Freedom From The Culture of Death

Author Dr. Joel Robbins' take on disease or *"dis-ease"* is defined as a lack of health. He states: *"Disease results when any cell is not functioning 100% of its designed duty whether due to trauma, toxicity, lack of communication or a combination thereof. Disease is due to stress. Disease is nothing more than the body responding to the wrong we have done to it. It is the body's attempt at keeping us alive in response to the wrongs we have inflicted on our bodies. If the body has the intelligence to produce a disease, it is capable of reversing the process to return to health once the cause is removed."*

According to the *World Health Organization (WHO)*, *"Health is more than the absence of disease. Health is a state of optimal well-being."* Optimal well-being is a concept of health that goes beyond the curing of illness to one of achieving wellness. Many of us have been brought up to believe that our health depends solely on the quality of the healthcare we receive and that the lack of disease is an indicator of health. The truth is, your health is much more than being symptom free and is your responsibility. You are the only person who can make the lifestyle decisions that contribute to your well-being. You are the one who must take the steps to preserve your health and promote your wellness. Only you have the power to create wellness for yourself. Your power lies in the choices you make every day on your own behalf. Your behavior and the choices you make in your life affect your health. You can choose to do more of what's good for you and the world around you, and to do less and less of what is harmful. You can choose to learn more about your health and the variety of healthcare options available. All of us have incredible inner wisdom. As you gather information and experience, you will gain confidence in using your inner knowing to follow your path to wellness.

For further information on choices for health and to get additional insight into how the culture is blindsided in the realm of the food industry, I would highly recommend Kevin Trudeau's book, *Natural Cures "They" Don't Want You to Know About*. This information will open your eyes and may come as a shock to those unaware of how organiza-

tions supposedly here to help us are actually hindering our well-being. In it he also talks about the reasons you are sick, the cause of diseases, secrets to losing weight and natural ways to cure yourself of virtually every disease. Everyone should read this book. Visit his website at www.natural cures.com or check our website at:
www.energeticbalancing.us

Author Catherine Ponder suggests, *"You must be careful what you notice, talk about, or give your attention to, because that is what you are identifying with, and that is what you will invite and bring into your life. If you notice, talk about and identify with war, crime, disease, financial problems, disharmony, this is what you are inviting into your own life."*

"What you can do to eliminate dis-ease from your life is start changing what you notice, what you talk about and what you identify with!" Reinvent a new possibility and express it. Talk about health!

Individuals who make certain wishes when in stress will most likely forget the wish or statement within a few weeks and dismiss it as a thought of the past—beginning a chain of events that require more than just traditional medicine and treatment, which can be something beyond their comprehension at the time.

Once a belief is received by the subconscious, it follows a straight path, sending a message to the immune system to enact the new instruction, thus the individual fulfills his conscious or unconscious goals.

The subconscious is a no-nonsense receptor of information which uses a simple, direct, precise and literal communication channel for programming, which the body sensing system receives. The level of communication to the subconscious is similar to that of a little child's means of communication. The subconscious does not make any interpretation, nor can it make sense of issues and/or subject matters. All communication is directly introduced at its' own face value. The subconscious does not determine between "positive" or "negative", it merely fulfills the command. The communication skills of the subconscious and the immune system are very primitive in terms of their transmission of the straight directions for programming. Nonetheless, the operating function of both systems is very elaborate and an astonishingly sophisticated process. The body terrain in which the immune system operates, is the single most important body system that keeps the body functioning in an orderly and healthful manner. The condition of a person's terrain is the element which determines overall health and whether dysfunction and disease will be developed and promoted. The state of being of the terrain depends on the totality of the interaction between the body (energetically), mind (beliefs) and spirit (cosmic). This interaction consists of and is either promoted or diminished by a number of factors, including:

- childhood conditioning;
- early childhood instinctive experiences;
- compounding and sustaining old beliefs;
- unresolved trauma and issues from the past;
- current lifestyle;
- victim mentality;
- level of communication with inner child;
- organizations, associations, and religious affiliations;
- type of nutrition, diet and environment (pH balance);
- activity, exercise and fitness;
- equally loving all of the body without discrimination;
- body harmony;
- life force and vitality level (chi);
- belief in mortality/immortality; and
- the basic, fundamental belief that you can control your life and that you are responsible for your own well-being.

Physical death is not a virtue, and for certain, it is not beautiful. If you are dying, you are unconsciously contributing to the death of everyone around you. Death is utterly unnatural—that is why it takes a lot of effort to die. In fact, most people exert so much effort in fulfilling the prophecy, that it, in actuality causes illness and pain. There is no reason for any person to age or die, unless that person believes and accepts the notion that he or she must die, just like everyone else. And society encourages the acceptance of this notion, for we must all be uniform in our behaviors, attitudes and beliefs.

The hardest part of becoming a true unique individual, who possesses dominion, an autonomous being who owns his or her distinct beliefs, lies in the act of making choices from options that are not accepted in our culture and may seem outrageous and selfish. The ability to choose is the utmost important option any human being can claim in his or her quest for self-preservation.

The ability to make choices which either promote life or death, will come as you understand that life comes in different colors. Choices which seemingly have similar paths may have opposite outcomes. Discarding the institutional (religious and government) myths and beliefs that pain, misery, judgment, and pretending are an integral part of normal and ordinary life, will be a must to do and to your greatest benefit.

Confusion

When confusion takes hold, we see only energetic charges that are around any issue in question, and we cannot touch and relate to the issue. We become "psychologically reversed" on the issue or the subject matter, and it becomes impossible to make meaningful and informed choices regarding that issue. In other words, confusion is a state of being, it is present about twelve months before the beginning of deterioration on all levels. A state of confusion can be prolonged for many years until you accelerate your death consciously or unconsciously, depending on your immediate conditioning and beliefs. You may even create a rabbit hole and follow it down to the other side. Confusion is a deadly matter, as an example—in a northern California community, where I lived for a long time, was the highest rate of breast cancer in the world, for women in their 20's, 30's an 40's. Everyone was buzzing to find out how this affluent community created this imbalance. Is it the water? Is it stressful lifestyle? Is it the high voltage electrical lines? Is there a vortex that is sucking the life out of these women? The government agencies are searching for blame. I knew many of these women—some were on my energetic balancing program.

In my opinion the source is confusion on all levels. Many women follow new age trends, giving their power away to someone outside of theirself in order to be in with the crowd, seeking "higher" knowledge from an "enlightened" source, rather than turning within. Furthermore, many of these women are vegetarians and consume soy products thinking they are a good thing. Soy products are very toxic and hazardous to your health when eaten repeatedly for over a period of time. I fully believe that the constituents of soy are a cause of cancer and hormonal imbalance. Such confusion creates a platform for an environment of misery and pain. When someone is giving up and buying into cultural beliefs, accepting only what is available as an explanation, there comes a downward slide into deterioration and a hastening of the death process.

As an observer, looking into the lives of the masses, and looking closely at my neighbors I see the disparity in the lifestyle. However, we all make our own choices, implicitly or explicitly. Most accept the cultural beliefs as a default mode, and are never concerned with taking a stand or making a choice. Most cannot see the choices of life and death.

Chapter 3

Culture of Death Benefactors

Desanctifying religion
The transformation in human civilization to a culture of death has come about with the monumental help of charismatic religious leaders. From the time of Abraham, the father of Western organized religions, to the present, organized religions have possessed extraordinary overt and covert control over its followers, and beyond.

In the name of God, organized religions have successfully unified national groups (countries and regions) under their particular beliefs, a sort of mass hypnosis to ensure indoctrination, in order to organize innately free-spirited humans.

I see religion as a combination of two most basic ideas: God and death under one roof, literally. In earlier societies and until the time of Abraham, the two issues were not considered significant or associated with one another.

Abraham was the singular and critical figure in bringing the concepts of death into the life of humans. From his time and down through all subsequent generations, life span and longevity has tragically shortened. Men and women began to die before reaching the age of 100, on average. The introduction of and preoccupation with the idea of death in society and in many cultures, perpetuated the acceptance of death as an absolute. But the fact is, that once an individual rids himself of the death belief from his body-mind, he also sheds the possibility of dying. Death is de facto a response to the acceptance of this belief. The death belief is the most fear provoking belief in a human being's life, and it has been given its strength as a result of organized religions having been firmly established in most societies. It is an institutionalized and accepted myth.

Before Abraham...his father, grandfather, and all generations born from the first man...humans lived longer than a mere few hundred years. In the Old Testament of the Bible, we see lists of many family trees by name and by the number of years the individual family member lived. The average life span ranged from 500 to 1,000 years. During these times, death was not a prominent issue in the lives of the population, death and old age were not a cause for concern in life. Those who died sooner than several hundred years, died in accidental mishaps, such as hunting, traveling unfamiliar territories, and natural disasters.

Before God was described and defined and streamlined in a uniform manner, each man and woman worshiped the Gods according to their own understanding. For them it was a very personal choice. As time passed, multitude societies were then manipulated into accepting the one God theory and relinquished the unique individuality of personal connection. In doing this, the leaders of these organized religions forced the acceptance of the belief in death as a way to come into the presence of God, to create group cohesion and deter to individual personal power. These beliefs were developed as extraordinary and invincible tools of control.

The structure and the system of religion evolved and grew in sophistication. Natural leaders continued to emerge, and they synthesized new and more elaborate notions to validate the worthiness of the membership, and determined what the membership must do to be acceptable to God. Religious leaders (and clergy) became the interpreters. In this position, they shocked and frightened the society into compromising their freedom by directing it into organized patterns of thinking for the security of a greater God. These altered forms of thinking and behavior slowly became integrated as acceptable activities that, in turn, unified the community as a whole. Folklore, legends, and myths were interpreted in a way which helped to carry and broaden the religious message. In these tales, the death belief became a pivotal element, and a concrete syndrome of fear was proffered in the way of storytelling. As a result, these glorious tales and colorful myths sounded believable.

Further, until the time of Abraham, the verbalized concepts of God were a pluralized word. In the Old Testament the name of God is "Elohim", which means "many gods", a representation of the power of that which created and sustains all. Incorporating all of the Gods into only one entity, establishing one power and one almighty God, followed. This faulty and dishonest act caused a tremendous shift in human thought, a deceitful one. With the power of one God in place, using "one", and with the assistance of religion, solutions were offered to humans—salvation was created and decreed for all of the needs of humanity. This concept of one God is a condescending lie that created the rift between creation and evolution and withdrew personal power in the minds of mortals.

These two elements, the establishment of a generalized, malleable syndrome of death in society at large, and the establishment of at least rudimentary forms of organized religion, mark a significant change in human longevity. Something altogether new and different came in. The modus operandi was to frighten people with the idea of death and then bring God to them as their savior. The leaders and interpreters of religious tenets gained astonishing power and control over huge populations. This is a fool-proof practice that works very well with humans, because we tend to use our minds to make decisions based on beliefs and purely mythological memory which that have no factual reality and which we do not question—it makes brainwashing a simple technique. A greater entity has been created that controls our life, eliminates our responsibility for our own life's outcome and to whom we are forever indebted.

To believe that you are nothing but a frame of time floating on earth, waiting to exit over to the promised land or world, where heavenly characters welcome you as a dead man, is actually one of the most destructive beliefs that a human being can hold. To be sure, God does not belong to organized religion of any kind—God belongs to and is

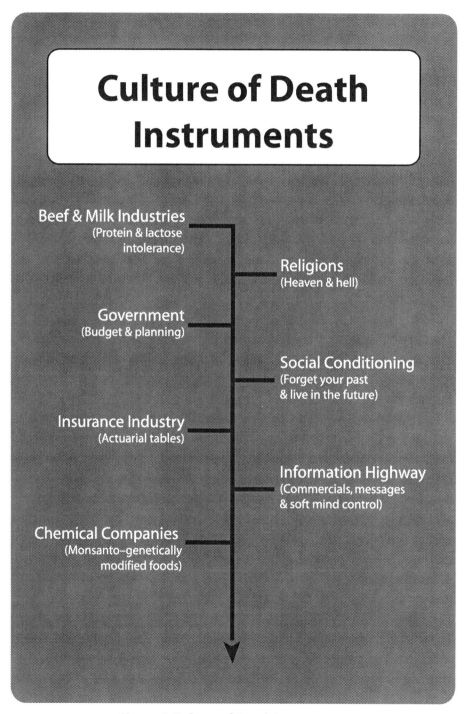

Figure 4: Culture of Death Instruments

present inside each man and woman personally and intimately. God is immediately accessible to you, whether you call out to him or her or not. Regrettably, all organized religions promote and base their beliefs on becoming a service provider for mediation and interpretation of God.

The acceptance of death as a natural event has become pervasive and totally ingrained, distilled and instilled in the human psyche. Religious leaders for thousands of years have been able to enlist the death fear, and the prospect of one's destination upon death, to frighten and control their membership. Indeed, throughout recorded history, the concept of death has been used as the whip to startle and suppress the psyche, often by using stories from the Scriptures that depict an end in death as a form of punishment for those who sinned. But, of course, there is a reward given to the believer who has behaved in accordance with the rules of the religion, and who has adapted and conformed to the expectations required. The reward is going to heaven, but first you must be dead, that is the ticket with the guarantee to enter heaven. And thus, heaven is not here on earth, but somewhere else far, far away, a place that can only be visited by those who has given up and checked out of life.

Social & governmental influence
All government financial forecasting and budget planning is based on mortality tables produced as a result of the Census Registration Act. Every ten years the government registers its' population in its new census count. This also tallies the number of deaths, which, in turn, influence and help balance the nation's budget. For example, let us assume that all Americans will live one year longer—the United States government will immediately go bankrupt. It is astonishing to realize how many public and private organizations depend on people dying as they are expected to. The entire infrastructure of ongoing social systems, as well as the allocated funds that maintain them, utilize census mortality rates for economic projections.

44   Ageless Living, Freedom From The Culture of Death

When one participates in certain cultural practices, such as the purchase of a life insurance policy, the depositing of regular monthly amounts of money into the maintenance of a retirement or "old age" fund, and even making statements such as, "all my friends have passed away", "I guess my time is coming soon", etc., there is a much deeper implication than we are aware of. These are examples of monumental doubts about having a long life, which rob the individual from any future or health. There is great power given to "the powers that be" with the present uniformity in society, where the goal of the community is to have a unified and uniform citizenship, that is, where all are and behave as a herd and as they are expected to. In this regard, everyone will predictably conform to the same future and the same end. To behave otherwise, is a dissension and unacceptable behavior. Such aberration is not well tolerated. Those who do not conform are seen as outcasts and outrageous.

Over time these concepts led to our present cycle of the perpetuation of death in the human mentality to a point where there is an inescapable circle of participation, the "death wheel", so to speak.

Some of the aspects of the culture of death include;
- no future;
- no vision;
- pain;
- no sense of possibility;
- slow death;
- denial;
- having no control;
- disease;
- pretending;
- judgment;
- separation;
- acceptance of religious control;
- surrender to government and bureaucracy; and
- being and accepting the "norm".

Symptoms of "The Culture of Death"

Sickness & disease

Pain & misery

No possibilities

Pretending & lying

Physical deterioration

Spiritual confusion

Figure 5: Symptoms of "The Culture of Death"

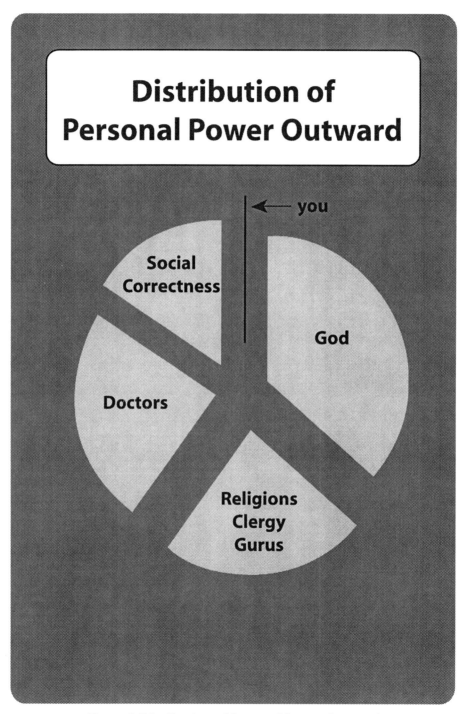

Figure 6: Distribution of Personal Power Outward

If the presentation of "the death process", as described in this examination of society, social and governmental organizations, is a depiction of your beliefs and judgments, and informs the way your life is flowing, then you are responding to a life and a future where you have already (subconsciously) given up on life.

The critical nature of choice

What are the critical choices? The most critical choice, before all others, is choosing life or choosing death. At first appearance, this seems obvious and fundamental. The choice referred to here, though, focuses on the ability to choose to live as an ageless being. We have never been given the option to make that choice because we simply accepted other people's ideas without questioning the validity of them. Just because people are dying around you, does not mean that you have no choice and must follow them. All deaths are chosen deaths. Nobody just dies, simply drops dead and dies. This is only a description of an event and we miss the substantive background leading to the death. Of course, nobody speaks poorly of the dead, and most speak of the deceased as victims. That is not the case, those who die choose to die through their beliefs that have accumulated throughout their lifetime.

Beliefs are the basic programming of the body and can be deliberately and specifically chosen and used as programs to replace those already established. The beliefs themselves are the blueprint of the body, which ultimately activate the DNA, which runs the body mechanism and the rest of our biological operation. The subconscious is the relay communicator and the protector of the core beliefs, which we collect throughout life.

Subconscious programming is normal and happens all the time. Nevertheless, there are different methods and ways to program the subconscious. Human beings are subject to an endless flow of information that is continuously surrounding them. Some of this is consciously received information, and some is subliminal, that is, directed toward the subconscious. A great deal of different forms of communication are designed to reach both levels of consciousness.

Primary Beliefs

Love & intimacy
Food & nutrition
Life & health
Death & culture

Acceptance without making a choice = giving up sovereignty & identity to become part of the culture.

cruising on default mode

Figure 7: Primary Beliefs

Individuals who have chosen to die make their choices and remain with them to the end. This direction can be altered or changed.

There are a number of ways by which to reach the subconscious and elicit change. You can do this through:
- mental communication—focused techniques/focused mind;
- body touch—various techniques;
- etheric plane communication;
- examining and clearing of traumatic events—mental or physical;
- positive use of mental disorientation;
- movement of energy (i.e. Kundalini awakening);
- activating the body into processing mode; and
- hypnotherapy—soft mind control.

Having chosen to change your life to be ageless, your new experiences cannot be evaluated or compared to your previous life experiences. The shift from a life of pain, misery and ending as a cadaver, to a life of possibility, future and well-being, is likened to a look through a tunnel that runs from where you stand on one end of earth to the exact opposite place on the other side. Nothing is going to make sense to you unless you are willing to expose yourself to your new options, fully knowing that only you control your destiny.

Working for 30 or 40 years for a retirement pension naturally gears the body-mind for death and brings nearer the end of your life. Do you see the hidden message? Being in this thought form and mind set is a killer in itself. Giving up on life is not a very nice thing to do to yourself. Who or what are you validating? More importantly, why are you choosing to buy into the "culture of death" philosophy? Taking responsibility for your own life is the primary condition and the starting point of your journey.

50   Ageless Living, Freedom From The Culture of Death

My use of the words "physical immortality" is a descriptive that is not ambiguous in its meaning. Namely, this means that you intend to live forever, without the possibility of death. That is the language that is necessary when affirming the new beliefs in life and to have them take hold in your subconscious. The best way to replace death urges, wishes and death belief frequencies from your subconscious is through direct deprogramming first, and replacing the vacuum with verbal programming and commands. The statements need to be delivered verbally, directly, precisely, simply and without the possibility of misinterpretation. Ambiguity may lead to confusion in the transmission of orders to other operational body systems as a direct response from the subconscious.

Pretending

The acts of pretense and imitation are two of the most negative abilities an individual can master in order to be deemed a functional person. In our culture and many others, pretense is a collection of behaviors passed down to children by parents, elders, heroes, "winners", patriarchs, matriarchs, clergy and trend-setters. We learn to pretend by imitating others who we see pretending and who we often admire. A good practitioner of pretense is sometimes considered to be an "enlightened" person. The individual is able to emotionally cover-up and mask many concerns in his life by pretending that he is mastering his pain and misery. When this behavior becomes chronic, it causes a severe debility to the individual. His social interaction is not free and open. It becomes a stressful exchange internally, where all energies are spent on image enhancement, maintenance or image reclamation. No wonder so many lose sight of themselves—they are not aware of who they are, but only identify with an image of themselves. Additionally, as the image predominates, their authentic and true inner strength becomes so distant and so unavailable to them, that it becomes a matter of life and death importance that the rest of the world see them as the image they wish to project. Image must be maintained at all costs.

Living in this culture requires that individuals incorporate the ability to pretend with proficiency, weaving pretense through every part of daily life. One needs to be, say, a good mother, a good father, a good employee, a good citizen, a good neighbor, a good parishioner—adopting the ideal role and pretense to match their perception of the part they must play. Pretending to oneself is a deflecting mechanism and often a form of relief from the constant drag of life, a way to distract from an underlying emptiness and inability to identify it. Pretending requires the psyche to adopt a foreign entity or shadow sub-personality to be brought forth from the arena of the collective consciousness.

To maintain pretense, it is important not to unravel the picture—the better the pretense is played out, the less exposure and revelation of oneself is revealed, which makes one feel safe. When pretending or role-playing, the body enters a state of confusion. In many instances, there is a fine line between the two states and which one is reality for the individual. In the mortality realm, the person who is not aware or conscious of the part he is playing will end up spending enormous energy looking for validation of who he/she is.

Unfortunately, pretending can go on and on throughout one's lifetime, or, to some point where a light goes on. This illumination will allow a new emotional opening by which to inquire into a different reality. The inquiry is usually a very solitary one. Those within the immediate circle of the individual who has begun to inquire have vested trust in the individual as they know him. A dramatic change in the outlook of an individual can cause social, emotional, psychological and personal disturbances in the people around him. Something new is often threatening and difficult to accept. When everyone "plays the game" in a social construct that encourages and rewards pretending, all become part of the system, participating and investing in it. It may be frightening for one to watch himself operating this way, especially when heightened awareness reveals a lack of change and denials.

Pretenders
Poem by Robert Sciarrillo

All about me are pretenders. They lie and they cheat and they steal and they ridicule and they hurt. It is the same everywhere I go. Deception, yet in all actuality, it is only themselves whom they lie to, cheat out of, steal from, hurt and deceive. For when one denies ones' self, when one pretends to be what one is not, when one must cheat, steal from, ridicule and hurt others to feel superior to ones' fellow man, one is merely deceiving one's self. One is hiding from one's own fears and short-comings. One is a coward. For a "Real Man" is in touch with his heart. He need not lie, cheat, steal, ridicule or hurt others. He feels no need and gains no superiority in deception. No. he is always true to himself and always follows his heart. He does not pretend.

Chapter 4

An Exploration of Physical Immortality

Introduction

Now we can begin to identify and describe aspects particular to individuals who live in the process of physical immortality. Examples of ageless physical beings do actually exist in this world. Entering this realm, one finds an intriguing and wondrous place. Most people, now and throughout all ages, have had thoughts, fantasies and knowledge about their own immortality. Living as physically immortal is a true and actual possibility. It is only a matter of choice that one incorporates this reality into his life and reaps the wide and spectacular array of benefits that are waiting for him. One simply has to choose to be "alive" during his present life cycle.

Is that all there is to it? Yes and no. Becoming a physically immortal human being is a pure and free option that is within the reach of anyone. You do not have to be wealthy, brilliant, gifted or saintly. If physical immortality is so readily available, then why are so few counted in the membership? The primary reason lays in the fact that world societies today are based on complete acceptance of and adherence to what I define as "the death process". Immersion in the death process only allows individuals to pretend that they are living.

Our present societies, and their mechanics around the globe, are based on this culture and system of death. Death, as the single most agreed upon reality across all segments of peoples, has become the underlying belief system that operates and orchestrates the human physical body. It is an unchallenged and absolute model of the completion of a life cycle. Right? The concept of death is imbued in our psyche practically from childhood or sometimes from the time of conception (as a result of living in the womb of another being with death beliefs for a period of time or by energetically imitating and adopting our mother's beliefs).

Throughout our lives, the belief in death has been introduced and reinforced again and again by parents, teachers, peers, organized religions, social and health organizations, and by the very lovers and spouses with whom we share our private and personal lives and often look to for support and validation.

To be defined as a productive adult in society requires that one follow certain rules and practices of citizenship which are established by the myths and the beliefs of the culture. It also requires that one does so without question. Yes, in the culture of death productive adults must eventually die, but these men and women have souls and spirits that will survive their physical body and will last for many lifetimes to come. Isn't that wonderful, now you can die respectfully and resign all your life possibilities to your next reincarnation! What a waste. This is a malicious practical joke we play it on ourselves.

Discussions in this chapter may cause you to reconsider aspects of your life and define your beliefs anew. Most likely, you will realize that the beliefs you hold have become more important than who you are. You will realize that you have expended an excruciatingly large amount of life energy (chi) in the vigorous need to protect and defend your beliefs? Why? Because they have become part of you, and it is frightening to consider something else. By the same token, you will also realize that you are able to get rid of them, like a pile of junk, or a tiny annoying tick that has been attached to the surface of your skin that can be pulled out and removed.

Here, I will suggest compelling, definitive arguments for a defiant decision making path regarding your future in this world. Living as a physically immortal being is possible and is achieved only when the belief in the death process is out of your body. Knowledge and contemplation of physical immortality without mastery and appreciation of the physical body is nothing more than foolish rhetoric at best, because

Chapter 4: An Exploration of Physical Immortality   55

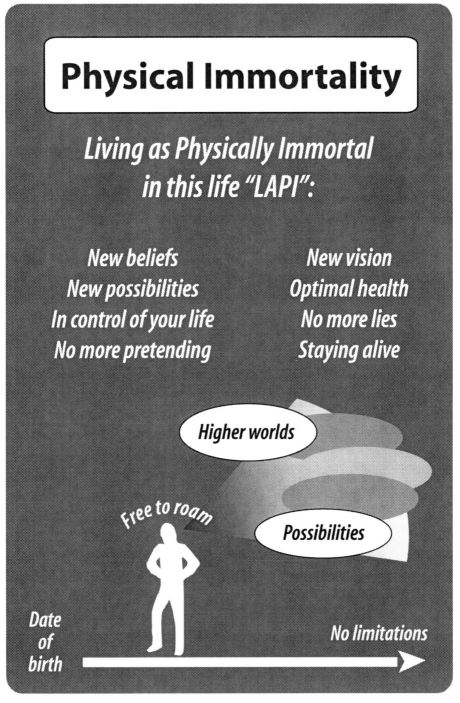

Figure 8: Physical Immortality

life and living can be manifested only by means of a well and whole body, which, of course, includes the mind, as they are one. There can be no future in your life beyond what society deems for you if you believe in death.

Here you will find new information upon which to base the expenditure of your life energy and explanations about living in the realm of physical immortality. These are probably totally unrelated and different concepts from those ever offered to you before. Entering into this realm of possibility will shake free your life's core beliefs in a way that you can live your life without limitation. You will be entering a space that is forbidden by society. At this nexus, you will need to consider your current belief system, your experiences and their origin. What may then emerge is an examination of their validity, merit and usefulness to you, bringing forth bigger questions: Who am I? What am I doing in this life? Is there a purpose to this life? Is there a purpose to my life? Do I really need to die?

A view of Immortality
The realm of physical immortality has no boundaries, and there is no right or wrong attached to it. This realm is all about options and possibilities, as ongoing changes are the rule. This realm will allow you the opportunity to unravel your death urges and free yourself from the culture of death environment. Entering the process requires no qualifications or need of approval by any other human being. There is no age limitation or restriction due to physical or mental condition. Registration is not required. After reading this book, you may accept physical immortality, practice it, or just entertain the concept as an interesting alternative thought. No judgment is placed upon the decision you make, other than your own.

Exploring this conversation on ageless living enables me to share my experience and learning, to offer you the knowledge that I have come to find in living my life as a physically immortal human being. This may sound a little corny, however, someone has to be the example and the storyteller. It is my hope that in doing so, this work may touch you in such a way as to raise your conscious awareness a few notches higher to build upon that level, bringing you to a state of oneness and unity with all the parts that make up who you are.

This process takes true introspection regarding life-long beliefs, and it takes lots of planning and follow-up to hold a commitment to being "alive" while the initial work is in a fledgling state. This is real work on yourself, not just mental hocus-pocus exercises. For, by now, you must know that mental wishes (affirmations) have no practicality in and of themselves. They may be characterized as nothing more than "mental masturbation".

The information and understanding presented here is based upon the experience, knowledge and information that I am always receiving as a result of living as a physically immortal human being. This knowledge and experience becomes wisdom as I continually integrate and utilize it. The accomplishment of evolving into a limitless being on other levels is obviously rewarding (at times it feels lonely). My world becomes lighter and sweeter with every day that I am alive! It is truly wonderful to shade the heavy input of messages in the environment, which bombard the psyche, mind, spirit, body and energy. It is truly exceptional to be unaffected by the flow of any negative influx. This intense debris of negative information no longer belongs to me or in my realm of experience. This type of understanding allows me to discern the sources of negative input, their messages and intent, and to stay clear from such influences. With this extraordinary advantage, personal transformation is incredibly enhanced.

Becoming a physically healthier person is a by-product of being in the process of physical immortality. Health is the result of a combined sharing of resources to keep the body operating at optimum condition. Utilizing and teaching methods, techniques and practices keep me at the level I am, as I move to the next level. There is no mark or final goal to reach—any goal is only a point on the path for personal advancement. There is no limit to the level and reservoir of your self-love, from which you love all others. And accessing a direct line of communication with your God-creator, without the need for a "middle-man" or a broker to facilitate this direct contact with God, is everyone's ability.

No limitation
The concept of "no limitation" is rather broad and can apply to all levels of human activity, from the functioning of the physical body to the interpretation of social practices and beliefs.

The awareness that one is living without limitation supports the framework for visions free of any boundaries. Within limitlessness, visions can create the basis for all the pieces that will then build our lives—thinking with expansiveness, thinking of all possibilities, all options, thinking in terms of unlimited visions. The only limitations that we have in our lives are the ones that we put there as part of our experience. These are the limitations that we have accepted and adopted, that have now become embedded deep within our body-mind.

Physical immortality is the philosophy of the "living". It is the only "cause" that you cannot die for. In truth, one can never achieve immortality—one can only practice it and live it to the fullest extent of possibility. You cannot purchase it, keep it, defend it, protect it or own it. It is an ongoing knowing and state of mind you can choose to practice throughout life. Physical immortality is something that you can enjoy as long as you live. You live as long as you enjoy living.

Eternal life is a state of mind that is the outcome of an inclusion of non-traditional understanding, one that is fed by an ever-present intuitive connection to common sense, and wisdom of the critical mind and life itself (higher mind). As you know, all beliefs are baseless—without any merit and proof as to any factual basis. Human beings tend to accept other people's myths and beliefs just because it exists in their reality.

It is common for people to limit themselves by making private or public declarations regarding different aspects of their lives based on unfounded beliefs or unquestioned understandings. It is important to listen to the statements that you make and see if the knower in you

Chapter 4: An Exploration of Physical Immortality

agrees with the statement. You may ask yourself, "does the source of this statement belong to me?" "Does this belief serve me?" It is a good exercise to question the validity of any belief, thought or opinion. What might have been appropriate for you at one time may not be the case now, even in the passing of one day. By now you have changed and grown in new life experiences.

It is relatively easy to identify the limitations in our lives. We can wonder about them and estimate their validity. To take charge to change a particular behavior can be very simple, without help from the outside. Here is the process and some questions to ask yourself:

- Think of and focus on a statement that you have made, often make or philosophy that you live by.
- Write it down and read it, so you understand it exactly. Then, re-read it to see if it is a positive or a negative statement.
- Ask yourself, "do I like it?" Yes or no.
- Ask yourself, "is the statement true, does it reflect my experience?" Yes or no.
- Ask yourself, "do I really mean what I have said?" Yes or no.
- Ask yourself, "are the meaning of the words correct and match the intended purpose of the statement?" Yes or no.
- Ask yourself, "does this statement accurately represent how I feel at this time"? Yes or no.
- Once you find what your specific intention is, then you need to change your statement to reflect your intention or reject it altogether.
- Visualize a new meaning and create an image or a symbol of it.
- Rehearse this new symbol or image in your mind.
- Exercise retrieving this symbol or image from memory.

Sometimes individuals lock themselves into a pattern of speech that does not really belong to them and is not useful anymore in their vocabulary. There is a way to use language to derive a positive outcome that now truly represents your thought or what you want/where you want to be. Once you imagine and realize the new possibilities in using a new word or statement with a new meaning, a mental shift has been created. That will help you to be aware of your pattern. You can use this reframing exercise all of the time, it works like a charm!

Being set in your ways is not a compliment to you. It is not a position of power from which to operate. "Being set" means that you are standing in one place. It means that you are not moving forward. It may also mean that you are spinning your wheels in the same place. Your options appear to be closed. "Being set" in this way, or that way, may be a comfortable place for you—it could be safer to hold on to the past without taking any chance in venturing into creating any change for the future.

The statements "I do not want to rock the boat" or "I can't find the time" or "It's the wrong time for me", are totally about being trapped, fearing life and not having the willingness to change and shift. Normally, after you hear this kind of statement from a person, count about 12 months into the future, and you'll recognize the beginning of a major illness or dysfunction creeping up. Nobody is too old or too young (if they are in a "living" mode), to create changes to manifest their inner wishes and desires.

To be physically immortal is to be in a space where there is nothing in this world that is beyond your limits. All things are possible to achieve as a reality for you.

The biggest limitation in life is the belief that you must die. This dying belief is directly ordering the DNA to start the "adaptation process" to biologically start destructing your body. If you hold to this belief, where can you go? How far can you go? The answer is not far enough. This belief will, to a greater or lesser degree, consume all your options and possibilities, creating a severely circumscribed future. You must reject the subliminal inducers that deepen the belief in death inside you. Truly begin to fully believe in yourself and the future you deserve. If you only remember when, as a little child, you had the feeling that you were going to live forever. Start to reclaim your intrinsic vision. Beliefs we harbor directly affect our biology, there is no separation.

In my book *Life Unlimited,* I presented the finding, and the concept that the human blueprint, or DNA, is based on the belief system rather than a solely genetic DNA as the blueprint. The DNA will change and adjust it's operation according to the specific directive of beliefs. The only cause that matters are your beliefs, which directly link to the effect—your biological response. In the near future this will be a common understanding. It is hard for the culture to accept this principle widely at this time, due to the influencing power of religions and the acceptance of the present paradigm, which both promote death as the basis for its existence.

Body cues
Once a state of limitlessness is realized, recognition in the body occurs, and the transformational awareness is integrated into the imagination. This recognition is physical and may be felt in the viscera, and, with many individuals, in the digestive system. This feeling, vague at first, will become more developed and more readily recognizable, as a signal or form of communication between the body systems, and the conscious mind. This communication evolves over time, to a point where it becomes a clear, instinctual inner body signal for the conscious awareness.

This acknowledged feeling and energy flow may be a response to food that you are about to eat, or to a person you are about to speak with or an image you find yourself fantasizing about. Whether sensual experience or simply mental (imaginations, fantasies, thoughts, visions, etc.) the effect on the body is identical. All, in their way, affect the physiology of the body-mind in the same manner, and with the same degree of effectiveness. For me, at times the feelings become like a signal, to receive a yes/no indication regarding the world around me. My heart sends a smile if he likes me to do certain specific things.

Bodily responses are often treated as unwanted functions. The body's way of making us aware of certain functions can sometimes manifest inconveniently. For example, the growling noises that the stomach and other adjustments of the body sometimes produce. Often one will suppress or try to prevent natural internal movements to avoid embarrassment. These noises are important releases—their suppression can be harmful and will hamper the smooth operation of synchronicity of the body viscera. The rejection of the feeling will also further distance that person in his ability to listen to his intuition and body communications.

Role playing

Physical immortality is a state of being, an operating mode in life. It is an unending process of life—changes are very welcome, accepted and a natural part of living in this universe. There is nothing static in the universe, all is flowing and moving and changing. Humans live their lives in constant change from one breath to the next. Physical immortality is the ongoing observation of life as it unfolds in front of you. You become a true and full participant in life. This is the most rewarding and fulfilling state of being that any human can reach. In this state, there is no limitation and no pretense regarding any aspect of life.

Pretense and role playing is a behavior common to most—it is part of the natural development of children, as they pretend to be their parents and other adults, or pretend to be glamorous heroes and heroines. We have also learned to act when things do not go right in our lives. Each person develops his own style of acting/pretense, of covering up, of separating from their feelings and emotions. Pretense takes the place of misery and pain through denial. This self-deception shoves the emotions deeper and deeper inside the body-mind. Pretense is one of the most widely utilized escape mechanisms usually adopted from childhood onward.

It is possible to live in constant denial throughout one's entire life without knowing the real person who lives inside. Sometimes it is difficult to face the stranger who resides inside—how can you explain the decisions that you made in the past that consistently denied your existence? It is not easy to face the grim reality of a life lived having never been true to oneself.

When you experience physical immortality, the need to lie or pretend about any aspect of your life is neither practical nor necessary. All new beliefs are received and accepted by choice. There is nothing to prove to anyone. There is no competition. You know that all of your "competitors" are merely living out their own life plan. This has no relation to you. What others think of you becomes irrelevant. This new place you are experiencing is beyond the concept of competition and beyond the maintenance of image. So, as you can see, pretense is for mortal men and women only.

Chapter 5:

Advantages of Physical Immortality

Wholeness
Wholeness is a state of being. Wholeness is experienced on three levels—physical (energetic), mental and spiritual. All three are entwined and inseparable, and are elusive if not based on the merger of the following three layers that constitute humankind—your inner child + present self + vision of future self = one.

As a humanist, I have found that the deepest and most compelling state of being is when there is communication between the adult person and the inner child. The integrative bonding that results, and the trust which develops between the adult and the child, constitute the fundamental basis for living in a state of wholeness. One cannot experience a state of wholeness without having the inner child clear, safe and absent of the emotional "baggage" that was so unfairly attached to her in childhood.

In my past work with hypnosis, I specialized in childhood trauma clearing and the bonding process. In my opinion, this type of work is most basic—all would be wise to consider a specific process of trauma clearing as a great tool for enhancement in moving beyond the mortality realm. In regard to this, I highly recommend beginning by freeing the inner child to the point that he or she feels safe enough to operate in the present dimension. I cover this in greater detail later in the book.

As an example, wholeness is a powerful state which you will acquire when both the inner child and the grown adult are in a state of safety, combined with a future-self which is very easy to design and compile for the future. When this state of being is achieved, you will gain awareness and enjoy a new inner power, a power that can effortlessly handle all the world has to offer. This inner power is very satisfying and evinces a great recognition of yourself. This is the highest possible acknowledgment you can acquire through your combined inner resources and identity. This inner connection is the ground from which you recognize your own essence. With wholeness in place, your vision of the world is constantly new and positive.

When wholeness exists, you are able to conquer both worlds you are experiencing—the inner world of self and the outer world beyond the self which, of course, is a reflection of the inner state. Because of the power that this consciousness creates, one's control moves from the inside to the outside, where the ability to be stronger than external forces is most magnificent and rewarding. It carries with it a new feeling of being able to control your own destiny and the outcome of events that are transpiring at the present time. Of course, this logically translates to the control of future events. Achieving a state of wholeness is possible and available to all.

Body-mind unity

As a state of wholeness is realized in its fullest dimensions, a new level of internal communication is reached that gives unifying character to an individual. This can be defined as "body-mind unity". Body-mind unity is established as the result of the changes that occur while clearing old trauma and self defeating programming. Once the changes take place in their entirety, one's vision of oneself becomes clear. This clarity reveals a free person who has come out of the past. An internal bonding is in effect among body, mind and spirit. Energy flows unimpeded and can be felt very distinctively as you become reacquainted with your original immortality urges.

Body-mind unity is the continuous interaction that occurs when both are clear and in agreement about their intention, both operating and functioning at the same level, by sharing the control of one dashboard (responsibility for decisions), while generating physical functions. The beliefs by which they are fueled are common to both, and operate at

Chapter 5: Advantages of Physical Immortality

the same level. A sublime clarity and flow of energy are evidenced—the mind thinks of an idea and the body will operate directly to produce that idea, it always has, the difference being that now it's creation by choice. There is no conflict during the transmission of the thought or order. The individual is in absolute and complete control of his inner environment. The response time from the body is very short. This is not likened to the autonomic response, but is likened to a highly developed conscious and subconscious. The communication becomes free, direct, fast, precise and uninterrupted.

One can ask the question: why not focus on body-mind unity as a step in the process of immortality? Yes, it is the first undertaking. However, to just focus in your mind as most normally do, positively affirm yourself, do a mental clearing, let someone touch your body or receive bodywork and have your enlightened teacher tell you all is cleared, and proclaim you are physically immortal, is not enough to create a lasting transformation to bring a state of wholeness. In most cases, the result is very shallow and within a short time may cause further confusion and disappointment in our abilities.

For deeper lasting transformation one needs to clear old programming and transform old childhood trauma and discontent. Two things must happen: the first, acknowledge and locate the stored issue. Second, remove or change the issue by creating a new positive outcome (program, belief, picture, understanding, trigger and response) to replace it.

I have met many people who consider themselves, as do others, to be enlightened beings, living or supposedly having lived on the cutting edge of spirituality as an advanced human, with an exceptional understanding about "humankind". Despite the state they have achieved, I know not one of these people yet that is not aging and dying or has not already become a dead teacher or guru!

My dear reader, there are no shortcuts when mastering your body. There is a need to deprogram the body from past conditioning and habits first and then to program the new choices. "The proof is in the pudding" only if the individual can perform in life as an "alive" being. All the talk in the world is merely a mental exercise. What matters, is the energy that runs the individual and the outcome of his life.

The process of LAPI can be developed and elevated, helping to transform the entire being without discrimination. Distinguishing special parts of the body and contouring as better or lesser, is fragmenting the whole, and that is the worst discrimination act of all.

The body-mind is a very unique apparatus that can alter its functions and adapt to new situations in order to maintain stasis and to preserve the body's survival, in spite of the numerous habits we sustain which create physical toxicity (slow death). The body-mind responds directly to beliefs even in situations where the beliefs and their actions are detrimental to the well-being of the body-mind. The physical body will adjust and abide by any new situation and new programming. What we learn from the body's behavior is, first, the body can accept poisons of all kinds and adjust its mechanism to facilitate acceptance of the poison. Second, the body and mind tend to become expectant of the poisons. I assert that all foods are poisons, and the body accepts them by degrees. If food as a necessity of life is part of our belief system, then the less food one will eat, the more energy and better overall existence one will have for longer periods of time (creating greater longevity).

The deterioration of our bodies, caused by the environment and lifestyle of modern society is ongoing if we remain in this conditioning. Reversing this trend is possible, feasible, doable and practical. This usually happens within a very short time from the day of your commitment to LAPI. The progress of the process is naturally a very individual one. A commitment to change is of utmost importance in order to overcome the negative influences of the surrounding culture.

Control over the immune system
The immune system is a direct function of the subconscious. Belief systems are the body's blueprint and consequently control and influence everything the body stands for. They reside in the subconscious and

direct the DNA. All functions and behaviors are directly or indirectly the outcome of what our beliefs are. This blueprint is responsible for the behavior of the body's systems and the outcome of the physiological responses. The beliefs that an individual accepts and carries within will determine the value, quality, and the future of his life. They determine the condition of his physical body.

When a new, more positive belief is accepted and adapted to replace an old one, the new belief will take hold and will re-imprint this new information directly in the new cells that are being produced in the body. Therefore, as the body keeps reproducing itself, it will have a new program to interact with. In an amazingly brief period of time, the physical body can complete the cycle of reproduction of the entire body with the new belief. This, in turn, will produce a new genetic structure totally different from the previous one. This new body will continue to be reproduced according to the specifications that the individual chooses. New beliefs shape the content of the blueprint and the desired results continue.

Once a new belief is installed and becomes a primary influencer, then greater changes will happen in the physical body in every subsequent cycle, about every forty days. Therefore, one can manipulate the functions of the immune system, and any other system of the body. Indeed, the power to change the functions and the visceral operations are not limited only to the physical structure (chemical and biological). This power extends to the energy system, specific mental functions, and the functions of the nervous system. The mental is the tool to create the change, then energy system and so on ultimately effecting the physical. As you can see, each person can become the production manager while operating his own body. Essentially, he can create any change that he desires to achieve.

The immune system communicates the same way as the subconscious (i.e., precise, direct and literal—it does not interpret orders). The immune system's job is to faithfully execute the orders given that "come down the pipe", not possessing the ability to question or interrupt the orders. There is no judgment of the orders or the commands when changes are desired to reverse a situation or regress certain unwarranted physiological development. It is necessary to communicate to the subconscious directly when installing a new belief for a new outcome.

Regarding this internal communication, a basic rule to follow is to love all of the parts of the body, with no objection whatsoever toward any particular part that may not be functioning correctly—i.e., disease or dysfunction. This rule applies whether in the physical or mental bodies, or when emotional behavior is the focus. There is no place for discrimination at any level of any system and function of the body-mind. Dissociation and disregard of physical parts, bodily responses, emotions, feelings, will elicit unwanted symptoms.

Once parts of the emotional body (sub-personalities, shadow personalities, entities and saboteurs) form identities and overshadow the essential self, these influencers will take charge of issues, causing illness and disease to form without being controlled. Rapid deterioration of functions and systems will cause further dislike of these parts, resulting in further reinforcement of the systems and escalation of any dysfunction. Actually, all dysfunction that occurs in the body is connected with sub-personalities or entities that are "taking it on themselves" to resolve the issue at hand in their own way.

Love is the magic word here. Love plays a central role in avoiding physical problems before they develop to the point where they become dysfunctional. Love can greatly assist in rescinding the development of certain dysfunctions.

Another basic rule is that one must embrace and love his disease or dysfunction, cooperating fully to resolve the issue that caused it. Of course, the most difficult matter here is the element of overriding personal blame, where one must transcend self-blame in order to acknowledge the situation and take responsibility for having formed the disease without blame. It is also easy to blame somebody or something else, or to blame genetics. It is easier to believe that the individual himself or herself had nothing to do with the formation of the disease. The perfect denial—if it is not yours, then you can dislike it. The more disease is despised and hated, the worse the disease will get. In this circumstance, the chance of healing is minimal to none. Normally, disintegration of the body functions will continue very rapidly. So, remember, love is a key word here and a key element in the healing process.

There are different techniques and processes to communicate with the body, to reconnect with it, and to mend all parts of the body. The integrity of the whole body is the desired outcome. Many researchers and practitioners in the medical establishment can see only the symptom formation and the dysfunction in and of itself. Most traditional techniques that are presently being used are in response to the particular part that malfunctions and its biological and chemical component.

Eliminating pain & disease
The condition of the body terrain is the outcome of the love and the care an individual gives to his or her body. In other words, there is a need to have communication at a certain level where the body-mind and spirit work together in harmony. The cause of all problems begins when disrespect of the body from the conscious mind reaches an unmanageable and unacceptable level.

Techniques for elimination of disease are based on the understanding that nothing happens in complete isolation on its own. As we discussed earlier, sometimes memories are deeply buried and virtually impossible to retrieve. We think that if we allow ourselves to forget what happened, the problem will go away. Unfortunately, the physical body remembers all too well. It is the parts of the body, the tissues, muscles, bones and organs, which carry and store memories too. The memories of the cells last longer than the cells themselves because the memory is also part of the blueprint for cellular replacement.

In order to regress or totally eliminate the development of a disease, the first thing is to find out what the underlying issue is that has become suppressed. Second, begin to work to pacify the concerned body part that is manifesting illness and work toward resolving the issue that was buried. After agreement has been reached between the parts, new beliefs need to be introduced and entered into the subconscious to replace the old beliefs that initiated illness. There are no miracles in healing, even if the doctors call it a miracle. It is their way of saying "sorry, my methods are not working". All healing is natural and normal to the body, and happens from the inside out.

The person who has been cured or whose condition has gone into remission did something or experienced something that happened outside of medical understanding. True, that person did do something that the other did not do—that person healed his own body by accepting himself as a whole, resolving his issues internally by working on them to the point where a satisfactory resolution was reached. Sometimes there are inner forces (guides, such as intuition, and untapped knowledge sources) that help in the search for the right solution.

Most people think that the physician's job is to keep you in good health. They think all they need to do is merely arrive at the doctor's office and tell him to get rid of their problem immediately. Physicians will continue to treat the "vessels" of pain and disease rather than their origins. For example, all headache pain is a by-product of the energies of unprocessed emotional issues. It is too bad that there aren't any instruction manuals for humans.

Pain may be physical, mental or emotional. All pain and misery relates to the limitations of options and level of possibility in the individual's life. The pain level rises according to the rise in the feeling of powerlessness to control events in life. There is understanding and mutual agreement (subliminal agreement) that pain is part of our life and we need to live with it. The teachings of organized religions maintain the death belief along with the belief that pain is a natural condition of life. This information is implanted at a very deep level inside the body and is even advocated in "spiritual" teachings.

Chapter 5: Advantages of Physical Immortality

To change death beliefs into life beliefs, by itself, is the first major step toward mental and emotional acceptance of a new reality. This is not, however, enough. The real task is to bring the physical body into a state of wholeness by making choices that compliment the complete body-mind. In this stage of development, a person can reverse any and all illness and disease having occurred from past behavior and thoughts. Any possibility of illness becomes nonexistent for an ageless being. Under no circumstances will the immune system permit a generation of dysfunction in the body when one vibrates at this level.

Once a level of transformation is reached where an integrated consciousness of body-mind unity becomes accepted practice, and wholeness is the basis upon which you live your life, the changes that occur physiologically are very profound and continue into the future with cellular repatterning.

Age cessation
When body-mind unity is achieved, the cells of the body will begin to reinvent their make-up to the cellular structures of a pre-symptomatic time. Their development will be more associated with, or connected to, the original structure they were at birth. This development in the cell can cause reversal of the aging process. When allowing the cell to reproduce itself according to the "new" blueprint, it is possible to heal any part of the body-mind for the better. Humans have the ability to reproduce or change the physiology of any particular muscle group or organ to meet their existing physical needs or demands. As such, when operating in this realm of possibility, the aging process will stop instantly upon the change in belief of lifespan.

As discussed earlier, disease development in the body is directly related to negative programming connected to the belief in death. Anytime the body reproduces itself, that is, generates new cells, aging is diminished. Internal directives are calling for cellular changes that permit health and vitality. In the simplest of ways, this makes sense. Changes can be profoundly stunning and can even occur over a brief period of time.

No more fear

Fear is a common feeling. Fear is a learned experience with a large emotional component. Once the feeling of fear is experienced, the body can reproduce that same feeling very easily. We are introduced to fear in childhood—in fact, most have felt fear as an infant. Fear has multiple levels of intensity, and it triggers emotional and physical mechanisms. The part of us that experiences the fear is normally the part of us that cannot do anything about it. It is the "child" inside of us, our inner child.

The inner child's influence on the functions of the body is remarkable. The inner child sets the tone, comfort level, determines the participating emotions, and behavior relating to every individual experience. The fear level is a response to how much comfort the inner child feels when facing a situation. The more comfort and assurance the adult person gives to his or her inner child for safety purposes, the more fearlessly difficult situations are dealt with.

By living in the realm of physical immortality, both the inner child and the adult have less to fear. Both aspects enjoy much more comfort and harmony in life, as they know that they are in control of their destiny and the outcome of their lives. Having a good relationship with one's inner child is a must for every human that wishes to live in a state of no limitation. The recognition and the validation of the inner child are imperative. In reconciling all the parts of the body-mind, an honest dialogue and communication is possible that brings safety and emotional confidence to the psyche.

Of course, some element of fear is always presenting itself in life—the issue, though, is how we handle the fear. One can face and walk through the fear. The fear disappears when the inner child is communicated with and given security. One then develops a formidable confidence and surety in his or her actions. The feeling is genuine, and from this source comes true power to realize one's unlimited possibility.

Chapter 5: Advantages of Physical Immortality

Joy, fun & vitality

Being in a space of unlimited possibility allows a view of life from the choices that one has selected. Fun and joy are the only choices!

All work must be fun and joyful to perform, otherwise it is not an option for one living in the realm of physical immortality. For such a person, work becomes an expression and extension of the lifestyle and the choices that have been adopted. Work takes on all of the characteristics of a hobby. Such a person identifies his or her work as an extension of themselves. Anything less is unacceptable. Having chosen to become physically immortal has so much positive energy and renewed vitality that it touches all aspects of life.

It is quite easy for a truly joyous person to think only positive thoughts, thus facilitating positive outcomes. The ability to have positive responses to events and positive results from attitudes in life is not naiveté, the person is actually able to derive a positive lesson from even a negative outcome. In keeping with this, it should be remembered that vitality is an inner response to being the master of one's life. When one responds positively to a situation, the result is understood and is readily assimilated. Self-judgment is nonexistent, thus, examinations do not carry with them self-recrimination. The person who knows and accepts himself in this way sets in motion openness between himself and others that usually results in understanding others better. Nobody can hurt him or his feelings. He is not counting on any other person to validate or acknowledge him. The power that exists within, and the love of self creates safety and confidence in whatever situation arises. There is endless vitality inside the body. This is a reflection of how one reacts to the world. Vitality, fun, and joy are mainstays in the territory of the immortals.

Participation in life

To participate in life means to be able to make choices, to be able to create new situations, and to be able to flow when others are stuck. To participate in life is to become innovative and resourceful in dealing with events and happenings. To participate means to put oneself on the line without fear, knowing that no matter what the outcome, you will be okay. You will always survive. An end to procrastination is the automatic result of being immortal. Fear of failure and defeat even before making an attempt is not applicable to the immortal person. In a very practical way, there is no need to even use these or other defeatist terms, as they serve no purpose when creating possibilities. No limitation is the common denominator that underlines every sentence or statement an immortal person expresses.

Fulfillment in life

Fulfillment in life. What does it mean? In order to have a fulfilling life, there must be a purpose to one's life, and the ability to resonate with it. A dichotomy exists between what can be called mortal fulfillment and what can be called immortal fulfillment. They are two totally different realms.

Mortal fulfillment is a life response to circumstances in which the individual has little or no control regarding the outcome of events in his life. Having never considered or accepted the responsibility, the individual does not have any control of his destiny in a conscious or positive way. In this realm, the individual forfeits his will and dominion to the common beliefs, practices, and values that his culture asserts. In other words, he accepts the beliefs and practices of the death culture.

Immortal fulfillment in life happens when one's direction and future are synchronized. Fulfillment happens when all the desired wishes materialize without too much effort and sacrifice. Life was never meant to be a struggle. Nonetheless, healthy effort and involvement is called for in order to achieve a goal or create wealth and success. Trade-offs do occur—that is the nature of things. The individual who lives as an immortal cannot lose sight of the fact that self-truth transcends all material gain. It is a natural understanding of things.

In the realm of physical immortality, an individual develops a clearer vision and the future becomes one with one's desires. As with all learned behavior and responses, it takes practice. However, the body is innately familiar with the new way of being, perhaps because it was meant to perform that way. The results are fulfilling enough to stay on the course.

Chapter 5: Advantages of Physical Immortality

Changes in expectation about death create change in the intensity of one's approach in life. Knowing that you are not a dying subject, the hurry and rush that existed before, the drive to beat the creeping end before its arrival are nonexistent. Being in an unlimited time frame is one of the greatest experiences a person can appreciate. There's no hurry. You always have all the time you need. You will accomplish all you need to without pressure and without anxiety. You know that patience, devotion, and love will bring to you what you desire. You know that living a satisfying, long life requires an accumulation of a certain amount of wealth—however, you also know that you do not need to, literally, "kill" yourself or your body for survival. There is limitless time to be successful and accomplished. Once an individual takes the pressure out of this formula, he can see that the world will work for him to accomplish his goals and wishes. Thus, money will follow him when he lets it happen. Wealth is truly not important on a large scale. Having and earning enough money to fulfill all of your needs in life requires a hobby, with the intrinsic joyous qualities that all personal hobbies have. Then most of the intention found in one's life is directed toward helping or serving other human beings, helping others to shift and move in a direction that will transform their consciousness.

Depriving oneself of material goods is not recommended. There is no need to lock yourself in a secluded place, monastery or become isolated in a desert or a jungle in order to recognize yourself and find out who you are. Doing so in and of itself will not necessarily advance your evolution as a physically immortal human. However, experiencing sensory deprivation in any form for short periods of time, as a learning tool, is always helpful.

One key aspect found in living as an immortal is the luxury of having no restrictions when it comes to maneuvering in the world. Whatever you do will be okay for you. You will get all of the results that your heart desires, even if the results come by means of a most circuitous route. Of course, the underlying goal is fun, joy, and a lifetime commitment to serve and help others as you contribute to lessening the suffering in the world. As a person in the process of immortality, you will have the power to create the right circumstances in the life of the person you are helping and the discernment to know when it is called for. This is a standard truth. And for you, the reward is fulfillment.

Purpose & essence of life
How and where can purpose in life be found? For a mortal person, this may be the most difficult question of all. When this person looks at his life in some kind of perspective, he usually sees a lack of accomplishment in his past and a limited future. In most cases, one becomes the victim of his own closure and his vision becomes so blurred that there is no true recognition of self, or his "future self," as I call it . At this point, his mind probably wants to split from his body. He will feel that his only purpose is to maintain the status quo and move toward death while working on creating memorabilia out of his past events.

When you live as an immortal, your life essentially becomes dedicated to humanity. You can see the need for fresh air and vision in the eyes of your fellow humans. Love, unconditional and absolute, becomes the bedding upon which you develop your character and offer your work. Knowing what your purpose is on Earth is as effortless as breathing air. It is being rechecked every time you breathe. The goal is to fulfill one's intended destiny, a destiny that will make the world a better and safer place, where communication on higher levels can be enjoyed, (both conscious and super-conscious levels—mental, kinetic, etheric, trans-somatic and instinctive) and will be common practice in the lives of humans.

Higher spirituality
As you are probably sensing from the preceding pages, through this work, major revelations about your life, your present operating mode and your future may be disclosed to you. For example, in a "death culture" the attempt to engage in "higher spiritual knowledge" is an ageless trend that is usually served up as the answer and solace to all the ills of the individual, as well as the society at large (here I speak of formal, organized institutionalized religions and "metaphysical" circles). You may think that accepting a "God" image, as it is portrayed in its

enlarged, unfathomable form, resplendent in its omnipotent and omniscient state, is a natural recourse, but you relinquish your own essential power to what is, in fact, a mythical figure. Indeed, this transfer of power has the most devastating of all effects when considering the preservation of the physical body. In addition, surrendering one's power to his "teacher" or guru is equally as disempowering.

Believing that you are nothing but a frame of time floating on Earth, waiting to exit over to the promised place, where heavenly characters are waiting to welcome you as a dead person, is one of the most destructive beliefs that a human being can hold. To be sure, God does not belong to organized religion of any kind. God belongs to you personally and intimately. God is immediately accessible to you, whether you call out or not. Mistrust those who depict God in any adapted way—they wish to sweeten the fears of the death syndrome—for, that is essentially what all organized religions promote and base their beliefs upon. Regrettably, the standard common denominators found in religion are "God" and death. They have become synonymous and inseparable.

Once you know that the messengers of "God" themselves are fake, ill programmed, and dying, a response of freedom of expression regarding the Creator can emerge. You have questioned the messenger and the message itself. There is no longer any reason to continue dialing any number or contacting any "middle man" in order to receive knowledge, when you can dial direct internally and experience firsthand the power of the Creator!

Speaking for myself, I have gotten very close to my Creator. For me, God is the Creator. The Creator, or Life Force, if you will, has a more direct link with the outer worlds that exist along with ours, and each of us can commune directly. It is difficult to acknowledge that one can communicate with his or her Creator, as easily as one can talk to another person—taking direct responsibility for this is called to issue. Letting go of all limiting beliefs and communicating directly with God is a very enriching way to transmit thought. At the same time, it reinforces personal autonomy and allows each person to identify and elicit answers regarding what constitutes the essence of life for them. You can speak with God any time you wish. It's essential to let the message get into the body-mind and know that you are God.

In the society in which we live, individual lives are regrettably limited in scope and options. Piercing through and stepping out of, the dense and thick cover of social restriction brings out a world of magic, amusement, new adventures, limitless possibilities, new forms of love, new creations, trust and inner power. Personal change also often entails feelings of emptiness and a sense that one is "unfinished" or "incomplete". The discomfort needs to be attended to with answers. Here a truly spiritual journey begins.

When a person says "I am spiritual", what does that mean? Does it mean that he believes in something? What is it that she believes in? Is it that he thinks he is now connected to something? To what or whom? Maybe he means that he has now accepted death as an outcome for his life. Whatever he thinks, it is my opinion that we all have our own truth about what it means, and what we feel serves us in life, whether by choice or by default. I have come to believe and understand that spirituality is not solely in the mind. It is a behavior which includes the physical body as the center. To me, being spiritual is having absolute freedom to operate in this universe as an alive being without limitation. In my eye's view, a spiritual person, honors his/her physical body as a living temple and would never engage in behavior which would sacrifice its integrity.

In the realm of the immortal, spirituality is the enlightenment of the body-mind. It is the elevation of the consciousness and physical body to the level of ultimate possibility. That is, bringing the body to a place of recognition, to a place of awareness, to a place of knowing the truth about who the body belongs to (taking ownership and responsibility). One must support and honor all of the parts of the physical body. That includes the emotions, imagination, thoughts, input and outcome of self analysis.

Chapter 5: Advantages of Physical Immortality

It is fashionable to be spiritually enlightened today. It is the correct thing to do, and it is a social advancement. For mortals, spiritual enlightenment usually means a new path, a new organized belief, exchanging the method but not the story. Humans have been known to accept new religions and philosophies as they come into vogue. They think they are better off with the new one. However, it is crucial to remember that all the choices that are available in society to date, are of the same common denominator, an idea or option that holds some belief in death. The eastern religions have a softer twist on the death concept. They are more permissive in their description of the afterlife, and they always have a sweeter ending in their myths. Eastern thought seems gentler. East or West, the death belief is still the death belief.

Heaven on Earth
Quotes from Charles Brown

"Heaven on earth is a great concept we are all familiar with. You have to admit it sounds wonderful."

"Some people think of heaven on earth as a geographical location-a tropical island, or in terms of a period in the past-a special vacation, or a phase in their youth."

"As long as humanity is harboring deep in its soul the belief that we are merely passing through, on our way to some better world, then we are never going to create a real quality of life for ourselves here on earth. As long as everything about our lives is seen as merely temporal, as just a stop along the way, nothing is going to happen, and people will not move to make a difference in their life."

"Are you waiting for God to come? Or waiting for the savior, or are you waiting for the messiah? The question is what is standing in your way for having heaven on earth today? Is it you? Or is it your God? Is it your belief?"

"The hell and heaven you hear about are not located in any other dimension. They're both right here."

"This world is going to be shifted by people who have changed their own bodies and lives. If you aren't an example-if you haven't closed all the doors to death yourself, then you won't move other people to change."

"Mortal man begins to contemplate the possibility of his own immortality simply by listening to his own original thought."

Chapter 6

Considerations for Physical Immortality

Introduction

There are many factors to consider in your process of physical immortality. Eternal life is one of the most beautiful of all human possibilities, and body mastery is virtuous and thrilling. The primary benefit for those who choose to live as immortal beings is the quality of life that emerges as a result of this new belief. From all that is offered, continued health of the body-mind is perhaps the most significant gain. While living in the process of physical immortality, there is no possibility that you will contract disease of any type. In the absence of the possibility of death and fear of the death syndrome, you relieve from your body the deepest self-imposed curse ever.

Aging is no longer an issue. The body-mind can, and will, with the proper continued directives, halt the aging process, and, in most instances, reverse the aging process. There is no limitation or restriction to the body's ability to rejuvenate itself to the optimum level desired. Since we have an ability to call on the mind and communicate with ourselves, by ourselves, it is only a matter of directing the right intentional programming, so that the body may respond in the manner necessary. Physical change may take time, it may appear not to be changing, usually, in most cases it doesn't happen overnight or as we expect to look. We all have different time tables.

Imagine yourself without the burdens of pretense and judgment when relating to others and to self. Life becomes much simpler to comprehend. The body-mind is clean and free of the surrounding environment's negative energy, and the influx of harmful and negative societal energies.

Being in the process of physical immortality refers to the entire life-process. It is a constant awakening, awareness, and wonder of the marvel of being alive. As a physically immortal person, I continuously process the unfolding dynamic of cosmic energy, which becomes part of my evolving motion. At the same time, I am one with nature's life force. To see and observe every aspect of any given event of experience is absolutely thrilling. Personal growth occurs naturally when in this realm, because of the assimilation of all the information that comes to me in the form of verbal messages, sensory experiences, mental pictures, images, and emotional responses—transmitted and directed into my consciousness. When new forms of information appear, there are many things that happen concurrently as part of assimilating that information. A belief system adjustment takes place. My skeptic part now becomes the director of operations. My body then receives the information directly, on a cellular level, and deals with it instantaneously.

As I research my stance in life, I become the scientist, the laboratory and the "guinea pig", all at the same time. I play all parts at once. I hold observation of my life, my beliefs, my soul, my inner world, my bodily organs (one at a time), as well as the energy that is running through me. The totality of this observation sometimes makes it confusing for me to know which hat I am wearing at times. Maybe it doesn't really matter. To maintain clarity, I will speak out loud to myself at times. Expressing my thoughts by way of verbal conversation is an important way of hearing myself and reaffirming my new ideas and beliefs, which will then be anchored inside my subconscious, and thus throughout my cellular body. My experience at the moment is only the present experience. It may not be the one my path will take.

My life has changed dramatically since I have come to live as a physically immortal human being. Sometimes I feel that this transformation has been orchestrated by the goodness of higher powers. There is no part of me that is kept idle or has been left untouched by this transformation. All that I am has been reconfigured into a new creation of instinctive knowing, being and feeling—as if there is a new set of rules operating a new range or scale, with different levels that I am now able to use automatically. At times through the years, I get more involved and pro-active in my own programming, or I hold the post and move "in the trenches" to solidify my commitment to life. Not always do I keep my eyes on the ball—at times I get involved in the relatedness of relationship, and I invest more energy into harmonizing than I care for. Overall I take my time and am watchful of my options and alternatives, and elect to choose from pure self interest. Doing so brings in divine intervention for the best outcome.

Regardless of your present situation, this information may counteract your old beliefs, cause you to condemn them and acquire new ideas and beliefs. Your sincerity and commitment to the dignity of the physical body, as well as the psychological and social aspects of it, will never be the same as before. There is no neutral stand for you to take. Your instinctive urges, thoughts, and senses, will be activated, and come to the forefront. Your mind and ego will play a big role in the way you will process information. Perhaps an awesome and somewhat frightening journey at first, if you stay on this inner journey long enough, it will become fun. Surely, it will be a departure from the mundane, boring futureless life that the world has offered you so far!

It is my deepest hope that the information herein will be as beneficial to you as the sun that shines and warms you from above.

47 questions to ponder
The following list shows the questions I have asked myself in exploring my beliefs. Perhaps you are asking the same questions yourself. Please take a moment to review the following questions:

- Do we really need to die?
- Who said so?
- What does that mean to me?
- Why do we believe in death?
- Who benefits from death?

- Is this only a belief?
- Is this belief genetically implanted in us?
- Can we undo the belief?
- Is it wild to think like this?
- Are we brainwashed?
- Why aren't we not doing something about it?
- This is not a joke, is it? This seems far out.
- What do we need to do to become an immortal being?
- Can everybody become physically immortal?
- Am I "over the hill" already? (Is it too late for me?)
- Can I reach this possibility even if I have a disease?
- Do I have to be happy all the time?
- What is the feeling of wellness?
- Is it ok to have possibilities beyond the normal ones? Beyond what I know?
- Is this thing for old folks only?
- Can I go against my parents' beliefs?
- Do I want to be different from my friends?
- Do I have to make a choice?
- Can I be both mortal and immortal?
- Can I go only halfway?
- Do I qualify for physical immortality?
- How does one know when one is healthy?
- Does this mean that one has no pain?
- Is it the doctor's job to keep me healthy or am I responsible for my own well-being?

Chapter 6: Considerations for Physical Immortality

- Do I have to get permission from my doctor to start becoming healthy and start living as physically immortal?
- Will my religious community approve of my action?
- Will they mind? I hope they will not disapprove of me.
- How do I start?
- How long will it take for me to be in the process of physical immortality?
- Do I have time to do this? I am so busy.
- I already have so many things going on in my life.
- Why are you telling us all of this?
- What do you get out of it?
- Are you the leader of a sect?
- Is this a religion?
- How much does it cost to be physically immortal?
- Is everybody welcome to start a new belief about living forever?
- Can I keep my old beliefs and add new ones?
- Will I be confusing my conscious and my subconscious?
- Is there a special drug to use that can help me change my...?
- Are you telling me that all I have to do is to think about living and disavow death in any form?
- Are you telling me that I have no life at this time?

Look at your own questions and speculations after reading the above list. Notice how limiting they may be. Find out what is missing in your life because of your beliefs. Change is a tool for you to play with, don't be afraid of change. If you are in a stagnation mode, notice what is holding you down and which belief you are reflecting upon and buying into at the moment which keeps you in this position.

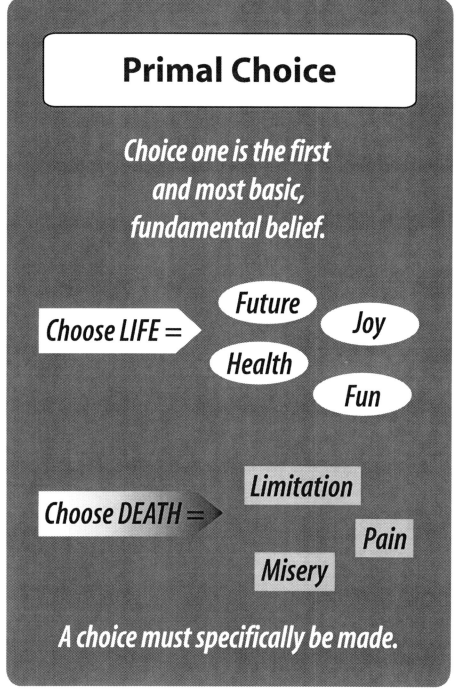

Figure 9: Primal Choice

Chapter 6: Considerations for Physical Immortality

Choice

Important life choices are made based on an individual's values and belief system. While the content of a belief may be arbitrary, and quite often erroneous, the motivation for choosing that belief emanates from the most basic of human drives: survival and pleasure.

Beliefs and values are very powerful. What else can possibly account for such noted historic events as Jonestown and Heaven's Gate, or, on a more global level, the submission of thousands of young men to follow the orders and commands of a leader who sought world domination? What is it about the nature of beliefs that makes a person surrender his essence and sacrifice his life? More profoundly, what is it about beliefs that make one human being feel so strongly about his own values that he or she is willing to take the life of another human being who disagrees with these values?

Furthermore, human beings are the only creatures endowed as free moral agents, possessing the ability to choose pleasure versus pain, thriving versus mere existence, whether consciously, subconsciously or by default. An individual has awareness if he knows what is going on around him in his environment. Although an individual may be technically aware of his environment during infancy, he is not fully and consciously aware of his ability to choose until later in life. Having chosen to survive, function and integrate into society, a person may find it necessary to deny and suppress certain feelings which those who influence him deem unacceptable or inappropriate, even if the feelings are of the purest nature. Interpersonal skills, including the ability to communicate with one's inner-self and with others, is a conscious choice individuals may make in order to have a greater vision and awareness.

Greater awareness ultimately leads to greater power to choose. Survival mode requires that an individual utilize defense mechanisms as a means of coping with his perception of reality. "Selective" amnesia is a method of exercising one's ability to choose to deny the pain of recall. A person's defense mechanism of suppressing selective memory is a conscious decision, or choice, to block or edit out memories of traumatic incidents, forcing these memories into the realm of the subconscious mind.

Motivation through choice is an approach to self-management that requires close individual attention. It means choosing to place the vision of oneself, and what one wants to have in life, as the primary priority. A person may choose to manage himself through threats and cruelty. Other conscious choices of self-motivation are to embrace gentleness, care and nurturin, or utilize kindness and encouragement.

Awareness for creation

Awareness by choice is a tool for the creation of personal power. One makes choices with awareness of their outcome and chooses to become aware of all aspects of themselves. You deliberately create what you choose and choose what you create within your physical life experience. Since that which is intended is of such importance to you, you have the ability to attain an understanding of a deliberate creative outcome.

According to Dr. Audre DeNard, "You create your physical life experience through your thoughts. Every thought that you think gives birth to a creation. The thoughts that you think, especially in reference to the things that you want, set into motion the creation and eventual fulfillment of what you want. Every thought, has creative power, whether your thoughts are creating what you want, or what you don't want." In other words, that which you focus upon, you will create!

Each and every thought is powerful. Any thought which is brought to mind regularly, whether with or without the presence of high emotion, will eventually manifest into physical realization or actualization. However, the thoughts that you set forth in combination with great emotion are the most powerful. The emotions that you feel as you are in the process of thinking propels and delivers into physical realization that which you are giving your attention to, regardless of whether the thoughts and emotion are "positive" or "negative.""

Chapter 6: Considerations for Physical Immortality

Creation by default occurs when you are unconsciously giving thought and attention to something you do not want, but nevertheless think about. Individually, you are the creator of your own life experience, whether viewed as good, bad or indifferent.

Within any conversation about soft-mind control, it is important to comprehend the power of the influence of others, since they may be stimulating your thoughts in a direction other than what you intend or want. It is important to physically remove yourself from any negative influence of others and protect yourself from their undirected, unfocused confusion and return your conscious thoughts to that which you do want. You must remove your attention, physically and mentally, from any negative or subliminal conversation.

As an independent human, you are the creator of your individual physical experience only, not that of others. You do a disservice to others by trying to take the responsibility away from what someone else has intended for him or herself. At this point in your development (beginner), concentrate on yourself. Only, when you master your own life, then it is optional to affect others into more harmonious lives. You create your life experience primarily through your physical conscious thoughts. The conditions in your physical life experience are the creation set forth by your own intense desire. You must begin and continue to make conscious, deliberate long range decisions. Your higher-self part will continue to guide you, even if you make decisions by default, standing ready as you begin to make more conscious choices in your life.

Chapter 7

The Path to Immortality

The element of wishing

Making a wish can be an action initiated merely for the fun of it. We learned to make wishes on many occasions during our childhood. Wishes can momentarily take us where we want to be to bring something or someone to us. Some wishes are referrals to things that are connected to the outside world—others depict a desire to gain or regain an object, for example, a missing toy or lost money. Once a child learns to make wishes and continues to wish, the ability becomes an outlet and a way of fulfilling needs.

When a person makes a negative wish or verbalizes a negative wishful statement, about an aspect of himself, things actually do happen. What takes place is: 1. The thought containing the wish will be received by the conscious mind and transferred to the subconscious, depending on how many times the particular wish is repeated, and 2. the "wishful statement" is heard by the subconscious, and thus the entire body directly.

When a statement regarding a death wish pertaining to the body-mind, is voiced once or repeatedly, the outcome will be detrimental to the well-being of the person. Most people forget that they have made such statements or held such thoughts about themselves. Within a few days, when their situation has perhaps changed or improved, they may entirely forget the wish which they made. The truth is the effect of the wish is still valid, takes hold inside the body, and precipitates a physiological and biological effect. At this point, no healing can occur—the catalyzing wish or events have been pushed deep into the body-mind for long term storage.

Evoking a death wish or some statement that carries a wish for death is the worst thing an individual can do to himself. Without exception, all such wishes will eventually initiate an illness or disease. Ironically, only two people in one hundred will bring to quick recall any death wish which has been uttered or carried in thought. Most will revert to denial and pretending mechanisms or will simply forget and suppress the initial statement, however it is not forgotten by the body.

Death wishes are sadly, very common occurrences. All types of wishes engender astonishing power in our psyche and become the transmission of requests and orders which reach the subconscious.

The main problem that arises is that the subconscious is listening to the words that have been spoken and accepts them as orders, only to pass the element of the wish to the rest of the body as a command and directive to the DNA to start an adaptation process. There is no such thing as having only joked about the statement that contained the death wish. As I have said, the subconscious cannot "take a joke"—it takes seriously and literally all information without discernment or interpretation—it is "the power of the spoken word". As far as the subconscious is concerned, it is simply a command and it facilitates the implementation of the request diligently. A basic death wish will promote aging and body deterioration in order to accommodate the wish for death.

Readiness for truly living
The qualification for true aliveness is living in the present. There is no age limit for starting the process of LAPI, and your physical condition is neither a hindrance nor a help—it's just the starting point. The fact is that as soon as an individual, even one with health concerns, starts the process, the act of being in the process will allow health to be achieved, in that the activities generated from LAPI will improve the condition of the body just by virtue of initiating them. LAPI is for everyone, without limitation. There is, however a prerequisite that certain conditions be worked on and cleared prior to starting the process: addictions and habits including smoking, regular alcohol consumption, drug use and abuse, compulsive eating, all considered suicidal conditions based on

negative beliefs. The purpose of this work is to promote the inherent immortality of the body and to elevate the importance of the body to its inestimable value. It is not okay, say, to smoke and at the same time to think you are preserving your body, this is a joke. Please do not waste your time and effort when you are not at a point of readiness. Not everyone's time is now to enter the process—you may not be ready. You may be ready in your next lifetime, if there is one.

I have met a few individuals who were very serious about the idea of living forever, but they continued to abuse their bodies. For example, to continue your habitual eating practices, having all the goodies you crave, while at the same time using only your mind to rely upon for your spiritual transition, is preposterous.

Accordingly, their bodies were confused by the opposing messages. I would call that pretending. Essentially, they are doing the same things that mortals do. They pretend that they are okay, while, through their behaviors, they are denying their existence and physical importance. Remember, the mind alone cannot improve or transform your body while you are in the act, however subtle, of committing suicide.

The preservation and rejuvenation of the body is one of the markers and a target while being in the process. When I speak of no limitation in your life, and say that there is nothing that you cannot do or become, I mean within the framework of preserving the body, which is the primary goal for existence. Destructive lifestyles are not part of the immortality process. When you meet a person who resides in a confused state, notice that their behaviors and their overt actions speak louder than their words. Be supportive and empathize with them, but don't waste your time on convince them to change—they are not ready just yet. And that is okay for them. Accept them as they are.

The dying guru
Some individuals may believe that their spiritual enlightenment and the beliefs of their group leaders, teachers, and gurus, whom they have accepted to lead them on the path of immortality, can transform them

just by the power of their mind, their "shakti" and their wishes. This is not so. It is easy to simplify the process and the teachers' message can be very appealing because it is very simple. They keep the followers interested and give them a feeling of creativity regarding their future.

The guru promotes the tendency to simplify and portray the objective based on spirituality only and to look to them for empowerment. The physical body then will always take second place. Working only with spiritual development, utilizing theoretical knowledge and myths, only contributes to further confusion and denial. It is totally a mental exercise without practical possibility to integrate living as physically immortal. In the early stages in LAPI it takes more work and diligence in terms of time spent, endless effort, and change in habitual functioning.

I question most of these teachings and the appropriateness for the student. If the Guru or the teacher is directing their logic to the sage, initiate, or a practicing physically immortal person, I can see a positive outcome. But to preach to the average person is merely an empty promise that again leads to more confusion and stress. This is another form of pretending and denial presented under the umbrella of "without limitation".

Placement of beliefs

It is my belief that in order to replace an old behavior or condition, you must first clear the negative issue, and then fill the old space with new programming. Overlapping an old belief with an intentional meditation or with positive energy by itself is not going to be permanent, just a surface cover-up that can create more confusion and uncertainty. Affirming and enforcing new programs must become a part of your system and a regular practice. Remember, you are reversing trends and beliefs that have been implanted in our species throughout thousands of years and have become a genetic code implanted in our cells. Please don't underestimate the negative power of the culture of death that surrounds you!

Chapter 7: The Path to Immortality

If you consider yourself a candidate for "living", and are truly interested in pursuing your life dreams and all the fantasies you've ever imagined, then you are at the right place. You will learn to become a very patient person, for patience is a mighty virtue and a basic and essential vision enhancer. Knowing that you are going to live forever and that time is at your disposal, you can start working on any item on your "must-do" list.

A gentle look at the process

How do you look at yourself? What do you see? There are many questions and issues that a man or woman faces when authentic introspection is conducted. None, however, are more important than these two questions. If these two questions are not addressed, chances are that little about yourself will advance, either toward forgiveness or acceptance and encouragement or growth.

When you are in LAPI, you are always in the process. You will never complete the process, and it is never over. As you are living in the process of being physically immortal, all conditions facilitate the individual in being focused and positively inclined toward all that living allows. LAPI makes it possible for individuals surrounded in this culture of death to achieve the highest fulfillment of being "alive" without limitation. That can be obtained only by participating in the process in a truly committed way.

When you engage in the process, and a higher awareness allows divine self-reflection, you can bring all of the above human expressions into a dialogue between and among all of the parts of the body.

Many people will be offended if you tell them that they are actually dying as they walk around, and their bodies are deteriorating from the material and non-material poison they accept into their lives. Death beliefs, along with products which are offered and promoted for us to take into our beautiful bodies, comprise the one-two punch that kills. One doesn't have to be a scientist in order to see what aspects of the external realm we allow to perniciously control our lives. Regrettably, most people have invested too much in their beliefs to be able to easily switch gears in full adulthood, without first making a strong decision and commitment to do so.

I have been mapping my life journey and have searched to find in the field of my experience a frame of reference, and principles by which to guide my life into the next adventure. My thoughts and understandings are unique to, and suitable for me. In the same way, your thoughts and understandings are unique to and suitable for you. I awake every day content and hopeful. Now that I live on light, I get my nutrition from prana alone (more on than off). It is another marker for personal freedom from cultural beliefs in food and nourishment. See more information in later chapters.

Knowing that I am in the process is the most powerful and self-sustaining element of my existence, since it allows me to love myself and other human beings with amazing ease. This is the most important part of having an existence that is "alive". Being in the process is the key to success for changing the "old" you to a new, young, healthy, confident, energetic, joyful, creative human being. This is not just a string of nice descriptives—it is fact when you chose not to be a part of the culture of death.

Groundwork for LAPI

In order to begin operating in LAPI, you must begin dealing with your most private issues regarding your ability to make a choice between life or death. Then begin clearing the childhood trauma and work toward becoming a whole person. Through this action emerges a greater awareness of personal goals and clarity of oneself. Internal strength is available to dissipate the impact of social and cultural agendas. You gain more strength as new beliefs adhere and become part of your daily life—benefits such as happiness, contentment, peace of mind, and unconditional love of self and others is the norm.

Unless directed toward creating these conditions, other disciplines and practices will have no lasting effect. These conditions are the groundwork for LAPI.

LAPI
A Must Do List

Clearing old trauma

Affirmation of new beliefs

Exercise

Nutrition

Cleansing

Therapies

Hygiene

Figure 10: LAPI A Must Do List

Sometimes an individual will become frustrated and may even give up the practice of a particular discipline of LAPI when no measurable results seem to occur. Despite this appearance, all work and effort will contribute to your evolvement and patience to remain on the path is fruitful. All the same, you have all the time in the world. When forcing yourself into a change in behavior or habit, as good as the change may be, a detriment is likely to manifest. Trust in yourself. You will change when the time is right. Period. You will change when you decide to change. Physical, emotional and spiritual detriments usually occur when the greater goal and purpose is out of the view, losing sight of the bigger picture.

The new experience

In establishing the groundwork for LAPI, it is important to feel free enough to take advantage of any therapies, traditional or nontraditional, that you may find helpful in your evolution. It is your choice to decide which one may be helpful to you. The idea is to achieve all of your goals, no matter how long it takes. And, for heaven's sake, use the therapeutic approaches that you deem responsive to your situation. Once you face and tend to the particular issues which are limiting you, you will find a wondrous feeling of contentment. It is as if you have finally discovered yourself and can have a real relationship with yourself. It is truly remarkable the way LAPI plays itself.

We have been told that all humans tend to have the same characteristics, that is, there are common behaviors that put humans in one group. However, there are many differences among individuals. To start with, the biggest difference is shown in the personal construct by which an individual defines his or her life. The critical factor lies in the degree to which the death beliefs have been implanted inside of you. The question is, do you recognize the two dynamics of the issue? On the one hand, can you identify your individuality and the life impulses that are part of you? Secondly, do you see the influences of the culture that have penetrated your body-mind and negate your primal life force? In all truth, most people are aware of this fact of influence, but succumb to the will of society, i.e., social consciousness. Many do not want to make waves or question what is acceptable as the norm. You must not be one who is concerned with making waves and should be willing to question what is.

Possibly the greatest challenge that you will need to cope with as you enter LAPI will be the occasions when you are standing in front of your friends and family and are called to stand your ground. They will look at you as if you are a lost soul or some kind of aberrant elitist simply riding another craze that will soon pass. However, you know that your journey is much more than that. More than likely, people will react to your new beliefs with reservation. Sometimes they may ridicule your ideas and proclaim your lifestyle a pretense or a cover-up of the real misery found in life. Their beliefs in the system are so strong that they will feel threatened and must play the game all the way. To consider this new understanding, the basis of their belief system would collapse, and they will fear that their "spiritual" standing and support will be lessened. A crack in their armor would result and they would be forced, if ever so briefly, to open their life to the scrutiny of their own skepticism. That will likely lead to a "near-death" experience, whereby they can replay all the events in their life, only to discover that they have not truly lived. And, of course, they expect you to validate their theme. Will you?

Chapter 8

Beginning Your Journey

Introduction

As previously stated, there are three dynamics which are viewed as critical to understanding and experiencing fullness of living: the role of choice, the capability of engaging in self-love, and the degree of personal determination one possesses.

The role of choice comes into play in numerous ways, but most importantly in the conscious act of recognizing and accepting one's present beliefs. Then permitting yourself to change or eliminate old beliefs and acceptance of the reality that the new choices will make, not forgetting that these choices will likely place you in discord with your peers. We have the opportunity to make life-giving choices every moment of the day.

Self-love is a personal source of power and a fundamental component to living a full life. When self-love is present, life becomes authentic, fulfilling and fun. Self-love is a normal, inherent quality humans are born with. Regrettably, things happen to erode it. Self-love is the source of all human essence, and the basis upon which all human relationships are established. Self-love gauges the relationship we have with our bodies. Self-love translates to inner power, vitality and success.

Determination allows us the persistence we need to maintain conscious awareness. Our determination strengthens our ability to fend off and discard negative cultural beliefs, especially death beliefs. We can work with, but not be consumed by, the information the world is giving us. We can use all the scientific advances of modern technology for the best possible outcome and not be weighted down or limited by it. In addition, a determined individual can be vigilant in continuing to help and support other humans in their various endeavors, and serving to help in relieving the pain and misery of their fellow humans. Determination clears the way for the use of universal laws to achieve the results needed to enjoy a healthy and successful life.

The approach that I advocate, teach and practice myself is a means by which to live in this world and enjoy the best personal effects possible. Learn about yourself. Get to know who you are. Accept and love yourself. Follow your own new beliefs irrespective of all others. Learn to "stay in the body", for that is where your answers originate. It is important to always remember to be "grounded". True, it is challenging to stay in the body spaces and operate from this basic level for long periods of time—most of us aren't used to it, whether we know it or not. The temptation to switch to the standard forms of escape from physical reality to the uncommitted ideas and beliefs of spiritual immortality only serve to limit the life experience.

We are alive for a reason. To diminish what is possible in life by subsuming our actions and non-actions to the so-called "nobler" realm of spirituality we will find after death is self-sabotage. In fact, it accomplishes the opposite! I believe no more spiritual person is an individual who fully and responsibly lives a life of vitality and awareness which integrates the physical and the non-physical. The idea here is to act from a basic level, using all of the senses, and operating from the body. This very simple concept holds that we see the physical body as the most cherished and valuable possession a man or woman has.

The question considered at this point is—are you a physical being who is having a spiritual experience or a spiritual being who is having a physical experience? What do you think? Can you honestly differentiate these two realities? Or, when are you in a sleep state, dreaming and fantasizing, versus an awake state, using the outer senses? Is traveling in the dream state the real thing? Or is driving in your car the reality show for you? Is it a matter of convenience to alternate, at different times, the prominence of one reality over the other? No matter how you answer these questions, when you are in LAPI, you may develop and acquire a new type of awareness of your actual totality—wholeness and oneness.

Immortality in this society
Surrender your critical mind, your logic and your engorged skepticism to the sound of your heart and to the melodies of your body. The mortal culture may think of you as a paler human being than they are. That is their prerogative. They are the ones who struggle with illness after illness and will end up dying. As you breathe yourself to life, they breathe themselves to slow death.

It is an apparent and welcome opening that our culture's progressive involvement in and fascination with a path of spiritual enlightenment is taking place. Extraordinary thinkers are helping us to understand the true spiritual self. Nonetheless, this appreciation of what is spirit in us should not come at the expense of the possibility of fulfilling the expansive enjoyment of life itself through the physical body. Actually, I believe that true spirituality embraces and respects living an authentic life, encompassing all of you in the physical form.

In today's society it takes a discerning and strong individual to accept complete responsibility for the majesty of a life that recognizes both the physical and spiritual realm. It is a unified realm in essence after all. Living as physically immortal places the responsibility of the quality of one's life square in the hands of the individual. I offer my ideas to you and make these ideas available to those who are at least minimally able to explore the possibility of living in their lifetime as physically immortal. My intent here is to challenge the old standards of belief that continue to diminish and circumscribe human potential and the basic, elementary enjoyment of life. Many people have no understanding that there is an alternative view of living, and therefore have no capability to integrate new points of view into their imaginations or challenge the validity of what society has prepared for them to accept as absolute truths. This situation is most sad of all.

In the last three decades, others have produced theories on longevity and have made public their views on the subject. Reading their works and examining their understandings have helped pave the way for me to integrate my own thoughts on this topic and gather enough confidence to bring my beliefs into my work in the last several years. Swimming against the current makes life quite interesting and challenging at best. The more I encounter needless pain and suffering in the community around me, the more determined I am to at least offer an alternative way of thinking about life to those who may be open enough to listen. Usually I present my notions on the possibility of living as physically immortal to individuals who are operating at a specific level of vibration conducive to openness toward the possibility of practicing LAPI.

Lists for improvement

To explore ways and means by which you can learn to help yourself on your personal journey, there are several methods offered below that have been shown to be effective and helpful.

Below I identify certain "elements" which one must reckon with in order to move into or through the process of LAPI:

<u>*Deprogramming and clearing of negative energetic charges to expose the real issues include:*</u>

- emotional clearing and trauma release;
- alchemical hypnotherapy;
- somato emotional release;
- biosync;
- re-birthing;
- breathwork;
- neurolinguistic programming;
- visualization methods;
- psychodrama;

Chapter 8: Beginning Your Journey

- eye movement desensitization and reprocessing (EMDR)
- emotional freedom technique (EFT); and
- programming and suggestions.

Synchronicity and balancing (skeletal, physiological, structural, energetic) methods include:

- neuro-cranial restructuring (NCR);
- atlas correction;
- scenar—little wings technique;
- somatic work;
- energetic balancing-(quantum prayer system 888-225-7501);
- manual therapy;
- craniosacral work;
- visceral manipulation;
- myofascial release;
- muscle energy;
- zero balancing;
- massage—non-invasive without oil;
- meditation;
- quantum touch; and
- Jin Shin Jyutsu.

Body cleansing and purification include:

- basic cleanses of organs;
- lymphatic drainage;
- colon hydrotherapy;
- parasite cleansing;

- oral hygiene; and
- H2O2 for oxygenation and other uses.

Breathing techniques include:

- breath awareness;
- deep, connected breathing; and
- slowing of breath.

Environmental awareness aspects include:

- pollution free air;
- water—clean and purified & organic food
- removal of mercury from mouth
- nature walks and observations,

Exercise includes:

- yoga;
- movement of any kind;
- jumping on rebounder; and
- aerobic exercise of any kind without strain.

Personal resources and spiritual development include:

- visualization of the near and distant future;
- sungazing practice; and
- dark room environment—cave-like conditions.

Things to avoid include:

- tv and radio commercial programming;
- talk shows;
- religious programming;

- negative music—abstain from "downer" music and depressive songs;
- life insurance; and
- cluttered living spaces.

Trauma clearing

Trauma clearing is a process where a person can begin to formulate a new interpretation of an event, which was traumatic and caused them to respond in a certain way to the traumatic event. Practicing this new interpretation will elicit a new emotional response that will now replace the old charged reaction. The new response will have a positive outcome when encountering familiar triggers.

There are many forms of therapies that have been applied for the purpose of clearing trauma, specifically childhood trauma. Accordingly, many books have been written on this subject, most of them describing and explaining the importance of clearing the trauma and its psychological and emotional aftermath. Practitioners and researchers from all types of disciplines, probably all in good faith, believe that their method is the best way to undo childhood trauma. Inherent in all of the therapies is the utilization of a method to bring the client to the exact place and time when the trauma occurred, as well as to encourage the surfacing of the recognition and the experience of that past event. But understanding the problem is only part of the solution. The trauma does not go away, but rather moves to a place of recognition for transformation. The process works from the inside out.

It should be understood that the methods are varied but the goals are generally the same. Some of the therapies can take many months, or even years, of intense work in order to reveal the trauma. Most therapeutic techniques apply methods that can go only as far as the client's re-experience and awareness of the traumatic event. Time is then spent with the client helping him to become familiar with the details, the story in its totality and the emotions connected to the event. At that point in time, (usually during a regression session), it seems the client feels relieved of the trauma, and both client and therapist believe there has been a clearing, and both are satisfied, thinking the session a success.

The reason I emphasize this specific series of events is because very few clients really achieve a clearing of the trauma indefinitely. It is my opinion that a few more steps in the process are required at the end of the therapeutic process in order to obtain a satisfactory and permanent change regarding the traumatic event. These changes will reflect a new outcome, a new meaning and a new interpretation of the event, via the inner child's perspective.

It is easy to clinically evoke and re-introduce the pain and the emotions of the past—however, to absolutely conclude the traumatic event, two things must happen. First, the event itself must be viewed from a new perspective and essentially reframed.

Second, the client and his hurt "inner child" need to communicate and agree on the same new view. An opportunity will therefore occur for the trauma to be owned, and then to be dissipated and released.

Bonding the child with her adult self is important for the purpose of acknowledgment, support, and mutual confidence in the understanding of the event. This must be done in the atmosphere of unconditional love for the inner child.

For some reason, a definitive conclusion to trauma clearing seems to be beyond the ability of many clinicians and therapists. They cannot seem to master such a therapeutic resolution for it. This may be due to the fact that they themselves do not have their own emotional clarity and unity within. Certainly, no therapist or teacher can take you to a place where he or she has never been. To achieve the completion I'm discussing, please refer to the above list for techniques, some of which I use in my own process.

Options to Improve the Quality of Life

All these Standard Options are deemed useless if you employ them under the beliefs of death that you accepted. The Standard Options may improve your condition only for a very short time.

Standard Options:

Sport
Exercise
Nutrition
Vitamins
Meditation
Therapies
Drugs
Consoling
Seclusion
Spirituality
Prayer
Religions

* Life Options *

Affirmation of new beliefs about life

Possibilities

Future

Love of self

Acceptance of the physical body

Renouncing the beliefs in death as unacceptable

Figure 11: Options to Improve the Quality of Life

Forgiveness

Forgiveness is an act of self preservation. It is one thing you need to learn and practice throughout life. Humans do not have good examples of forgiveness and have not been taught the act of forgiveness. We live in a society that promotes "getting even" and name calling. There is no forgiveness chapter in the U.S. Constitution. When an event happens in our life, and many will, we assign value to the event as good or bad. When we perceive or experience an event in a negative way, there is an energy attached to it which will grow over time, overtake and energetically effect our present lives and how we operate.

This can be the cause for energy blockages and disharmony effecting our behavior and emotional stability on all levels. Forgiveness is about releasing the negative feeling you have about an event. In other words, this is the same as releasing the negative charges that we hold onto for dear life. Negative charges are so destructive that they overshadow all new options and possibilities in life for as long as we harbor them in our mind. These negative charges will shadow your vision and distort any view of resolution. We create negative charges from any event where we were not able to learn a lesson from the experience. Forgiveness is like completing and divorcing your past behavior and putting to sleep the monkey inside your head.

During my workshops on physical immortality, I teach advanced techniques on how to undo and clear negative energies. If you have not forgiven your past and accepted your present, then there is not much for you to go on to be truly living. You are ultimately buying into the culture of death and experiencing psychic pain all the time. At this point make clearing work the center of your life until you can visualize yourself where you are the center of the picture, standing there with a big smile, without negative charges around you.

Deprogramming

In order to change direction, one must bring limiting beliefs into awareness and conduct a program of elimination of negative and self-destructive thoughts and beliefs.

Chapter 8: Beginning Your Journey

Our human development up to this point reflects the social acceptance of myths, and beliefs through the media channels and family traditions that originated from organized social structures, such as religions.

The methods that are used in our culture to program a person to accept certain beliefs without question include:

- mythology;
- story-telling and folklore
- power of the authority figures
- congregational gatherings and events
- imitation—behaviors of parents, peers, etc.
- media indoctrination—radio and TV advertising
- mass hypnosis—concerts and revivals, etc.
- trauma-induced mind control
- repetition—sermons, holy texts, etc.

These methods are in use every day in our culture. Seven of these methods are applied as standard techniques utilized by organized religions!

From this list you can see that these methods of programming are integral parts of our lives. Such phenomena have been inseparable from the basic human developmental process. In fact, many of the beliefs are instilled by subliminal messages as a result of observations of the cultural media and by way of buried messages flashed inside normal conversations. Once an individual accepts a belief, he must act on it. It is actually difficult to negate a belief that causes you harm, because of the body's ability to manifest directives and consummate the purpose of the belief. You can see how beliefs can be tough, rooted and a menace.

To undo a belief you will need to use the same methods as the ones that helped install it. When all the components of the body are in sync, it is easier to overcome and get rid of unwanted beliefs. Once you are able to link with and communicate well enough between the systems of your body, it becomes a matter of repetition to replace a belief.

When you are replacing a belief you need to be clear about your new belief. It is very important to be very specific, direct and certain of your undertaking. Uncertainty may lead to confusion and loss of direction.

When changing a belief, be sure that all your components are supporting your action. If one of them has any objection, then the transfer becomes shaky. The decision to choose and commit yourself to be "alive" must be unequivocal and "carved in stone", so to speak. Simplicity, directness and clarity are essential elements when undoing a belief or installing one. When you are about to undo/install a belief by yourself, be sure all the parts of you are in agreement. Sometimes you need to repeat the undo/install process more than once (see page 86 for clearing techniques).

A key element in this production is to be aware of the forces in the outside world—they have a tendency to sneak up and slip back in to take hold again if there is confusion. Once you get to know these outside forces (the outpouring of the culture of death), you begin to become watchful and vigilant to protect your survival mechanism. Sometimes it is just pleasant to observe the dynamic flow of the interaction and notice yourself and all the outside forces at play.

Communicating with yourself can take the following formats:

- thoughts—etheric plane communication;
- ideas;
- imagination and fantasies;
- body cues—viscera responses;
- thermal energy fluctuation—basic biological and emotional temperature.
- sub-personalities' conversations—all your parts.
- talking to yourself—verbal, out loud.

Chapter 8: Beginning Your Journey

Conversation and personal engagement with guides and entities may take the following forms:

- talking to your inner child;
- becoming aware of your intuitions—hunches, inner knowing, inner voice, gut feelings and mental flashes;
- connecting with the DOW—the divine one within—I get most of my communication with the cosmos here; and
- receiving and exchanging information with the consciousness grid—universal energies—this is the main connection to all there is.

Talking to yourself as well as answering out loud is an elevated form of communication. You need not judge or concern yourself about this. Talking to, or reassuring yourself, or any part of you out loud is acceptable behavior. In fact, this is quite normal and perfect despite societal admonitions. Kids normally talk to themselves, other beings and objects, at least before society fully programs them to cease the behavior.

When you talk to yourself, it is easy and rings true since only you know yourself and the original feelings which prompted the conversation. You know the issues firsthand—your voice is more convincing and true for you, and your body is familiar with your voice. You are the most reliable person to give and accept a suggestion or statement that really means something. Believe in yourself.

Every thought we think, positive or negative is a conversation. Every word we speak is a directive. Every action or behavior we take is a response. This is true because our thoughts create our reality.

Programming power
The way we live our lives is the result of a program that is already running. We live in a world of programming and programmers. In this world the programs are the safety net where we operate and within which we feel safe. As long as we are energetic beings, we operate much like a programmable computerized device that can write its own

programs and has the ability to design and improve at will all the old basic programming that is already in use. The fact is, we are a very sophisticated device with unlimited abilities to intervene on our own behalf and take corrective actions for self preservation and expansion.

A program I found in one of Jasmuheen's books which I highly recommend :
From "Pranic Nourishment", page 177

> "Your body is a bio-computer, your thoughts are the software, and your life is the printout of the two. Change the software, rewrite or modify the program, and change your life. It is that simple. Through conscious creation, via tuning and programming, we find Universal Mind speaks to us as we plug into the Divine cosmic circuit board. We are free from the need of food or sleep, from suffering for our divinity as we consciously program in joy, grace, ease and more. Awakened and empowered via intention, programming and playing by the rules of the Divine game we create a bridge between the worlds, between paradigms, and experience the Oneness in all."

> "Positive paradigms can be created by specific, intentional programming. Programming is repetitive instruction. As the physical and emotional bodies are governed by the mental bodies—higher and lower mind—in each "now" moment, effective programming frees us and also directs us through life. It allows the journey of survival to be simplified so we can then thrive harmoniously."

Programming I used myself, adapted from Jasmuheen's work and modified to fit my needs:

- I call forth all my body elementals and consciousness, and now command my Divine One Within (DOW) to;
- complete all my learning from past and future lives regarding abundance—I ask the DOW to remove any blockages within my fields that are stopping me from receiving all the abundance that is mine;
- guide me in each moment of each day so that my life will enhance the planet and that I feel nourished by being here;
- arrange all circumstance around me so that I may forever be free from doubt;

- surrender all my relationships to my DOW with the intention that my relationships are brought to their perfect level of expression so that we may be free to live our lives to our highest potential;
- let each and every day unfold in complete alignment with the divine will, that all my sharing in each moment is for the highest good of all;
- bring clarity and focus into my actions & behavior regarding life choices and nourishment.
- enhance my connection to the spirit world, to receive and learn about my action as human.
- let every cell of my being, on every level, mirror perfectly the divine perfection of the universe; and
- bring me all those with whom I can have a mutually beneficial relationship, NOW.

A story—my early days

At one time, I was too young to understand basic concepts of life. I hardly could speak or express myself verbally. I was lean and slim as a boy, about 38 inches tall, shy with minimal communication skills. Looking back to this early time of my life, I am amazed by the stand I took. It was my natural instinct.

Instinctively I was repelled at the basic idea of someone controlling my life, and that I had to obey a higher order. At home and in school, my behavior was considered unacceptable and unnameable—I had my own ideas of "being" and that was it. Lots of names were attached to me, like a rebel, fakir, or just stupid—for sure I was an inquisitive and stubborn child. At five years young, my family had just relocated to a new country and I had to learn a new language in this new evolving society, the state of Israel.

I felt much pressure to conform to the new situation. My world was spinning from possibilities to explore in my new environment, this new living place on the outskirts of Jerusalem. Behind our apartment building, there was a bare field and a trail that led to a rock quarry one mile further into unknown territory. I spent most of my spare time at the quarry, playing with the rocks, talking to them and enjoying the solitude of the quarry crater—it became my fantasy land and fortress.

At that time, my dad, a hard working and dedicated parent, did what all good parents will do, to indoctrinate his children into the cultural beliefs. This was my introduction to the real world of programming. It happened while my father and I were walking the mile distance to the neighborhood Synagogue on a Saturday for the morning prayer. As I walked beside him, he turned toward me and asked if I believed in God. I was surprised to hear him talk to me, since he rarely conversed with or talked to me, and I could count the times he did so from day one.

I remember searching my mind and trying to come out with an answer, but I could not, I had no reference, understanding or knowledge in my mind to give an answer regarding God. I knew it was an important question, based on his demeanor and body language. So I delayed my answer, trying to buy time to figure it out. I had a feeling that my answer would be important. I felt the gravity of the question in the air—my walk slowed down and I began trailing behind him. I was hoping that he would ask me another question or get distracted by something so I could avoid giving him an answer. Without luck, he was anxious for my response. I said that I was not sure about God, I did not know, I had not met him yet.

In my mind I visualized the Rabbi who always rolled his eyes upward—I thought that it was very weird and scary to see the white color of his eyes when he rolled them up and I wondered why he would do such a thing. My only knowledge of God was through this strange man who rolled his eyes, and I did not like it. I definitely knew I did not know if I believed in God, and I said so. My father's reaction was fast, with anger and disbelief that I would question what was expected to be a sure thing in his mind. He called me names and reasserted his dismay about my stupidity, telling me that I had no future, and that I would surely be a failure throughout my life. His eyes seemed to darken and they were focused on me like a laser beam. Then he grabbed my ear and twisted it so hard to the point that I felt it would rip my head at the seams, and he kept the grip for a long time, until he got tired. But the verbal abuse was more painful than my ear. At that moment, I told him I would never go to a synagogue again and I ran back home to my fantasy land at the quarry. After this episode, as a punishment, he did not talk to me and avoided any contact for approximately the next two years.

Growing up, I had to learn all about the culture I lived in. It is important to know what the culture expects you to become, the values, behaviors and socially accepted beliefs. While growing up in Israel, the number one program was that the country was more important than an individual's well being. That it is okay to sacrifice your life for the good of the state. Serving in the army was a mixed blessing. On the one hand I was happy to be away from my family and experience independence, on the other hand I had a hard time accepting orders on all levels, and I questioned everything that came from any rank higher than mine. I had to do much readjustment to fit in and became a borderline participant. At age 17 I knew that I must go beyond the limiting beliefs of the Jewish conditioning and programming. I was introduced to a book called *"The Knowledge from Above"* by Rudolf Steiner. This book introduced me to metaphysics. I joined the Israeli group of parapsychology based in Tel Aviv. The group met in Jerusalem every other week to study Steiner's doctrine and theosophy. We practiced with Ouija boards and performed séances. I was cautioned by my father that getting involved in this kind of belief could hurt me emotionally and mentally, sighting the quote from the Kabala, which states that only after age forty can a man start to look into the unknown or the unspoken world, as opposed to what is. Ironically, after forty years of programming in the culture of death, there are very few who can shift in "mid-life" to a new progressive possibility such as physical immortality and breatharianism.

Ageless Living, Freedom From The Culture of Death

Growing up in the land of honey, milk and olive trees, is all about entrenchment in the past and memories of negative events, with all the depressing stories about death and destruction through the history of the Jews.

Living and growing up in this culture colored my views and visions of future possibilities, with it's negative past, and it inhibited me from forming new choices and possibilities. This is a very basic cultural soft mind control that all societies in the world use to indoctrinate their citizens.

After coming to the USA, I wanted to go to school to learn more about metaphysical studies. I read all the books I could get my hands on. The more I learned, the more I started to realize that this was just another belief system. In order to be part of it, one needs to play by its rules and accept it as their own, another piece of dogma. Metaphysical beliefs are more interesting and are open-ended and come closer to touching a greater truth within ourselves. However, regardless of the philosophy and the background story of the belief/religion, they all end up with death, which I reject outright as an option for myself. Thus my journey began.

Chapter 9

Methods & Practices

Self-healing
What is self healing? Is it learning a trick? Is it taking the right amount of pills after you've done research, or is it learning your own biological system in order to understand the bodily functions, to learn the body map of meridians and so on?

In this culture, self healing is normally a conversation about disease and dysfunction. Regardless of who your therapist or healer is, you yourself, the doctor or the shaman—they will all end up giving or prescribing to you some form of remedy, hoping to change the balance in a specific system in your body. As long as something is taken as a remedy, this is not self healing. Self-healing requires a total change in lifestyle, especially in the emotional body. I do not consider taking any substance a resolution, but a way to affect one level of disharmony with another. The way I practice self healing is by not being ill to begin with!

If you are living in LAPI or on light and truly love yourself, and have gotten rid of the death urges from your body, then you can heal all. This means using directives for the mind-body to get with it, and to balance the impeded energy flow. Self healing, or healing of any kind, won't happen if you have not gotten rid of your beliefs in death, or left any unspecified reservation for the afterlife, reincarnation, karmic belief or understanding. Nothing is going to happen regarding healing or self healing nor will you realize any long lasting results if you've left any door open for uncertainty. Throughout our history, of all the masters and world renowned healers of any persuasion, there have been next to no real living examples of healing. The moment death occurs, the experiment has failed. The ability to shift and change your body's water content, or to change anything about your body, is real mastery and can happen only if you are totally living in your power of love without limitation for the future. The option for self-healing needs to be a clear-cut choice, without ifs, ands, ors, buts or maybes. In summary, true self healing can occur only when you can prevent a disease to begin with. All other definitions of self healing may be called temporary self healing or living in remission with this or that dysfunction. When an individual is in a state of wholeness with balanced pH level, there is no chance for any disease to flourish or take hold. Let me emphasize that these moments of a wholeness state can be the norm and long lasting, only if you have gotten your death urges and death wishes out of your system, from every cell within the body.

It is very simple and easy to be healthy. Clear and stay away from any toxic information that creates negative resonant frequencies which overwhelms the entire body. For me, I have been practicing my methods for clearing death urges and wishes from my body for some time. I pay attention to focusing my intention on more clearing in the body at all times. When you are healthy, you do not spend money on medicine, lawyers, therapy, drugs, vitamins, food and nutrients.

At some point on your journey, you will need to claim your sovereignty and stop seeing therapists. The day you do this, you truly begin your healing process. As part of my physical immortality workshops, I teach techniques for clearing death wishes and urges yourself, among many others.

The breath
Breathing is more than just a mechanical function of the lungs, it is essential for life. We can go for long periods without sleep, food and water, but only a matter of minutes can pass without life-sustaining breath.

The content of the breath, its quality, frequency and the fullness of oxygen being absorbed inside the body, will determine the vitality and longevity of each individual. Govindan (1993) writes at length about the significance of the breathing apparatus of the body and how it affects the physiological function of multiple systems, beyond the ones that are recognizable and familiar to us.

The act of breathing can be a voluntary or involuntary act. Breathing can be controlled consciously by the mind or operate as only an autonomic function with other viscera. Breathing is an important life function that can connect or bridge the mind and body, influencing both in many ways. Common breathing patterns tend to reflect our emotional and mental states. When angry, one jerks his or her breath, and during periods of fear, momentarily ceases breathing. Gasps of breath occur during moments of amazement or surprise, and breath can choke during episodes of deep sadness. The breath forms sighs of relief, and is slow and steady during periods of concentration or relaxation. Breathing always changes when one is thinking and imagining.

One can use breathing to master control over the mind and emotions directly. The medulla, the brains' majestic center at the top of the spine, is the governing entity that regulates the breathing operation. The quantity of oxygen in the breath determines the body's disposition regarding vitality, energy and life-force, as well as all of the body's physical reactions and psychological states. Life is not possible without a sufficient quantity of oxygen, and by deep breathing, we draw energy from the universal reservoir of life—the energy that holds the "life-force". It is both found in the air that we breathe and the sunlight that appears in our natural environment. This life-force is also referred to as prana. Prana is the singular most important element we need to acquire and use for basic functions as human beings. It sustains us, whether we know it or not. I have personally been living on pranic nutrition for the past five years. Though I do eat at times, I do not rely upon food for sustenance. See information on living on light in Chapter 12.

When we count the number of breaths we take per minute, we can calculate the amount of oxygen that the body and cells are receiving. The faster the rate of breathing, the less oxygen is received. There has been an increase in the breathing rate through the centuries, which by now, is averaging about 18 breaths per minute. The higher the rate of breathing, the faster the body deteriorates from lack of oxygen and "life-force".

An individual who can increase and maintain a sufficiently high level of life-force can continue living indefinitely. Note that the span of life is directly related to the rate of breathing. By slowing down the respiration rate per minute, the lifespan will increase as a direct function of this slowing down.

Learning how to breathe in a healthy manner can redefine your future existence. At present, there are not many places where you can go to study breathing techniques. However for those in the western culture, learning a new way of breathing from the practice of yoga is highly recommended. If nothing else, slow, deep connected breath will be sufficient and create a world of change when practiced regularly. For further information on raising your life-force and vitality level by another means, see "Energetic Balancing" and the "Quantum Prayer System".

Posture, energy & what it reveals
The position, the physical outline and the arrangement of one's posture (spine) reflects the state of being of an individual. The entire spinal system is the antenna to the brain. Continuous fluidity in a linear fashion of the dura matter is the key for proper body function. Each man and woman has a special, unique and highly individualized posture profile and pattern. One's posture tends to reveal the energy or degree of life-force the individual possesses. All humans have a definite ability to project and emit certain energies to the outside world. All living beings transmit outward 24/7, energetic information in the form of resonant frequencies, among other subtle energies. These energies enter into an exchange, are affected by, and cause an effect on other human beings and the entire universe. This energy has been given a variety of names, such as aura and vibration, and can be photographed with the use of electrographic photography. This outgoing energy is a reflection of the entire energy flow of the body.

Chapter 9: Methods & Practices   125

When observing an individual's physical outline, two indicators emerge that can be of therapeutic value in determining their true state of mind—energy output and postural profile. The postural profile can reflect the state of being of the person, that is, the state that the individual is experiencing at that particular moment, as well as their past and depth of belief in the death syndrome. In other words, one who is alive and self-confident will carry an erect posture, and one with low-life force (resignation, apathy) will slouch and carry himself in a constrictive way.

From my observations in my work with hundreds of people, checking their life-force and perceiving the energy flow of the body in relation to the physical, emotional and mental issues they carry, I have come to the realization that in our society we are greatly unaware of how we carry ourselves. The bulk of energy in our body is mainly carried via the skeletal system, therefore a healthy, erect posture is very important for conducting energy flow. In addition to the skeleton, there are another five layers of energy flow in the body. Pathways which allow a smooth, unimpeded flow of electricity and subtle energy is optimum.

When looking at profiles, you can see and discern numerous different types of postures. There are those with a very straight back and neck, totally erect. On the other hand, some profiles will show many different levels of imbalance—the upper back and neck bent forward in different positions, with shoulders slanted downward and forward, etc.

The body possesses points of energy like vectors that can be measured between them. If you measure the distance from the point of T1 to the point of the bellybutton, that would be one profile measurement. The second one is the measurement from the third eye to the tip of the cocxyc. These two lines can represent energy flow velocity in the body. The greater the distance between these points, the more efficiency in the flow of energy.

I would highly recommend that you seriously consider focusing upon correcting your posture to be as straight as possible, with the neck becoming the highlight of your body. The center of your neck is the diamond you carry and should always show. That in itself will cause you to automatically straighten your spine.

In showing your neck, with an erect spine, in addition to the perfect energy flow you will have, the position of the brain lobes will shift and become situated more horizontally and will therefore change how you process information. Maintaining a straight posture will affect your presence in this world and bring more certainty and confidence into your life. Also, with your neck showing and your back erect, you will automatically breathe deeper, more naturally and about 20%-50% more oxygen will reach all parts of the body.

On a personal note, I enjoy my posture at this time, having worked on it for many years and feel the effects of good energy flow and a sunny disposition. Keeping a good posture causes me to feel that I am the tallest person there is in this world. Walking erect commands an inner attitude which creates attention and respect. It is not how tall you are, it's how tall you feel!

For breatharians, those who live on light, and people who inherently have a slim physique, I strongly suggest that they also focus their intention on having an ideal posture, which will shift the appearance of being a "skinny" person to a perfectly healthy person. For taller individuals, this is quite important due to the length of their spine. You do not need to bend your body or your neck when you speak to someone shorter than yourself. Always stay erect whether standing, sitting or laying down.

As a small test, take one week to observe another human's posture. Try to eliminate any other information you collect about their personality. Do not judge the conversation with them, only their profile, concentrate on appraising the posture. You will be amazed how much an individual's carriage reveals about her!

Exercise

Why exercise? Who needs exercise? Exercise, as I present it here, is the employment of physical movement with the specific intent to condition the physical and mental body. In today's world, it is helpful to elevate the body's physiological and structural integrity in order for the body to function at or above basic performance and at a level where the typical stressors are easily dealt with.

The advancement of the mechanized world has shifted focus from physical activity to the convenience and efficiency of computers, television, video games, internet, automobiles, etc. This shift into the use of automation in all fields has created a plethora of new trends and cultural behaviors that have become accepted as unilateral improvements. These improvements have theoretically raised the quality of life, but the trend has created less and less demand for the use of the physical body and its' intended fundamental design for movement. Work and it's achievements have become the goal and focus in the lives of the majority of individuals in this society. The lack of daily use of the physical body will cause a deleterious effect on all aspects of the body's function.

We need to keep in mind that we live on mother earth, she is our hostess, and being here implies that we can manage and handle living with its gravity. Gravity is not to be taken lightly! The pull of it is a major restraining force that effects and shapes our body. Gravity keeps us attached at ground level, causing certain stressors on the entire complexity of the body systems. We are adapted to living here with this condition, and therefore we need to understand the significance of the effect on our bodies. In a way, being and living on earth is the greatest restriction to our lives. It limits us on all levels of our being—we become dependent on gravity entirely for all basic functions. In regard to exercise, gravity pulls down the body's outer layers, and can damage the unsuspecting fascia and skin. It's important to keep ourselves active, using and exercising all the muscles in the body without exception, with the gravity effect in mind. One can practice inversion, headstands, etc. to counter the effects of gravity. It can make the difference in looks and well-being.

The shift toward less physical activity is a pivotal event that will likely continue to influence future human development. More people seem to accept the limitations of their own bodily condition as a "fait accompli", often advancing their mental and spiritual development as a device to escape their failure to deal with issues related to limited physical capability. In knowing that the body is deteriorating, individuals tend to feel safer when they engage in and focus solely on advancing their mental and spiritual development. They dismiss the need to sacrifice any of their maladaptive habits or addictions that may take them out of comfortable patterns based on their beliefs. They simply allow their bodies to lose merit, so to speak, and sacrifice their bodies' intrinsic viability as a functional object. When the body starts deteriorating and losing its own system's credibility, a shut-down of essential functions occurs, and this shut-down hastens the death process, or the aging process as it is called by Western culture. Society tolerates this view of life and portrays it in our external reality as a normal form of living and being—the body naturally deteriorates and accumulates dysfunction.

The conscious act of movement and exercise can bring the physical body back to its proper condition and functionality. Movement takes shape with many different types and methods. All forms of movement are considered exercise, regardless of the type or method used. All people living in a modern society need to exercise on a daily basis. It is important to keep the body in good shape, and this offers a great deal of direct and indirect benefit.

Exercise will result in better:

- vitality
- mobility—free movement
- body conditioning
- body toning
- personal satisfaction
- openness
- self-acknowledgment
- self-appreciation
- self-love
- intimacy (all types)
- physical health
- body-mind unity
- oxygenation
- joy

All types of exercise are useful and encouraged. Use your common sense and gauge your progress by what your body is telling you about its capacity. When exercising, always take the long route so that the changes will be permanent. There is no need to hurry—you have all the time you need for achieving your goals. Become focused and persistent, and this will bring you the results you wish. Procrastination is not an acceptable option. Doing the smallest bit is better than nothing. And as you move along the path of your process, tending to the well-being of your body will stimulate other accomplishments along the way. A good-looking and feeling body brings satisfaction to the soul and spirit. The world responds to you more favorably, and human interaction is facilitated. A healthy body is a beautiful place for a happy mind and spirit.

Your mind's awareness of and attention to the physical body's ability and dynamic need to function at the best possible efficiency is an important marker in the process of living as physically immortal. To capture that awareness is an important step in and of itself. Observation of your physical essence and viewing it as an isolated element helps direct and keep your focus on your life's purpose.

Age reversal
Reversing your biological age is a conscious and intentional undertaking—90% of the practice is clearing the old beliefs of aging out of your body, specifically moving them out from each and every cell. Once the deprogramming commences, you can bring on the new beliefs as a vision and as a conversation with possibility, filling the body with new directives and total intention to halt all aging, and start the reversal.

The medical and scientific world looks only into the bio-chemical aspect of the body, which is less than 10% of the body's material content. By doing so, they overlook the main electronic device that manages the operating system of the body.

Devising new pills and new nano-technology to tweak the cells, is not the answer for longevity. All the exercise in the world will not help one iota if the body is engaged in the death process, which it normally is and there is not much to be done. Aging and death will occur almost on schedule.

All the genetic manipulation, "magical" anti-aging pills and nutrition are just a waste of money and time, if one isn't looking into the beliefs which they hold—it's a meaningless exercise in mental masturbation. There is no room for shortcuts when dealing with beliefs. As I mentioned earlier, our beliefs equal the blueprint of our body. All our genetic resources, DNA, RNA and chromosomes, are directly related to the beliefs we acquire and harbor deep inside our bodies. Beliefs, whether positive or negative are translated as symbols, and are energetically stored in the body as resonant frequencies. The storage of our beliefs creates new electrical links to the organs and the body becomes acquainted with prevailing beliefs.

Our bodies always follow beliefs with their respectful actions. The body does not rationalize and has no mechanism to offer any judgments or dissent for or against any beliefs. When the body is creating dysfunctional directives from our beliefs, it will inherently isolate the dysfunction it created, and automatically protect the rest of the body from the energy blockage that is constructed.

Exercising the body is important, to the extent that it has to coincide with the new beliefs about the vision of reversing aging. Exercise alone will not accomplish the reversal of age, but used in conjunction with new programming, it will. We all need to exercise in order to maintain agility and flexibility of the fascia and run energy flow through the skeleton.

Yoga

The word yoga means "union".

The practice of yoga is more than just exercise. It encompasses the working and healing of the body on six major planes of existence:

- physical
- mental
- spiritual
- intellectual
- vital
- energetic

The practice of yoga greatly helps in the gradual stripping off of layers of negative conditioning that an individual has acquired in life.

Kriya Yoga consists of a series of techniques which are grouped into the following categories:

- Hatha Yoga—affects the physical body & energy flow;
- Kundalini Yoga—affects the vitality (breathing);
- Dhyana Yoga—affects the mind (mental);
- Mantra Yoga—affects the intellect; and
- Bhakti Yoga—affects the spirit.

Practicing yoga dramatically improves physical health and well-being, increases mental concentration and clarity, and serves to balance and calm the emotions. Practicing yoga with purpose and dedication can truly open the road to spiritual enlightenment of the individual.

As part of LAPI, yoga is definitely on the "must-do" list, as one of the fun parts of the process. For the beginner, you can start with any type of yoga. Learn one method, and then go on to learn Kriya Yoga. Yoga, as practiced in the Eastern world, is connected to a collection of precepts and philosophy, which, in my view, aren't necessary or important in your practice. In my opinion, yoga techniques are the most profound form of body conditioning there is.

Ageless Living, Freedom From The Culture of Death

The practice of yoga is available to everyone, not only the fit, the gurus and their followers. You need to take advantage of this wonderful discipline and this resource of vitality for your own reasons and your own good. Remember, it is your obligation to use what you need to improve the physical body!

Hatha Yoga can be the perfect starting point. Twice a week may be an easy schedule to introduce the practice. Practicing yoga is not hard work or difficult. Within one month of practice, you can tremendously improve your body-mind's flexibility. You will be surprised how well your body moves and how great you feel. The practice of yoga may be an adaptation for life, and there is no need for fancy equipment or machinery. You can take it with you wherever you go. The practice of yoga is especially beneficial for men and women in recovery, who have a history of disregarding their bodies.

Chapter 10

Moving into LAPI

Markers of physical immortality

Here, you are offered a series of "markers" that may be considered focal areas where personal changes may occur as one begins his or her process of living as physically immortal. It is not important what is deemed as your starting point-you can move in any order you like within these areas of focus. Once you are committed to personal change, you have already started the process that will eventually lead you to the flow of living an ageless state of mind. You need to be totally committed to your life, without wavering. You cannot do this work for any other reason other than to improve the quality of your life or to enlist the internal power within to identify the purpose of your existence. One great indicator will be an inner feeling that your heart is smiling to you, reflecting approval of your choices.

Some individuals will shy away from this reinventing work because they consider the opinions of other mortals as more important than working toward experiencing life in its optimal glory. This response is just fine, not all seekers are at the same level of personal awakening. The choice is one's own in the final analysis—a life that allows you to be healthy, happy, confident and in control of your own destiny, or a life that is fraught with limitation and early death.

Using the structured principles of improvement that are presented in this book will help you to understand some aspects of a "to-do list" that, in turn, will help you to "jump-start" your life as a truly alive human being. Do not expect to conquer all obstacles immediately—it is better to spread out your personal program so that you may allow enough time to be your own lover and healer. Time becomes of no importance the longer you are in the process.

The following list describes specific tasks (in no specific order) that require attention and accomplishment to be in the process of physical immortality.

- clear and own the past;
- communicate with your inner world;
- create a wish list for improvement;
- visualize future experiences, events, and goals;
- breathing readjustment;
- unconditional love and respect—for the inner child;
- self-love and acknowledgment—for the adult;
- listening to your body with all the senses;
- acceptance of the belief that you will live forever; and
- unconditionally rid yourself of the belief in death.

Regarding specific attention to the inculcation of the death syndrome, I offer the following exercises, which I include in the workshops I lead on physical immortality—to help you remove the accumulation of death wishes and death urges from your body from a cellular level.

First, I do a journey meditation as an exercise and teach a specific technique to delete and undo all death episodes and experiences that you have had throughout your lifetime.

Second, I take you on a journey into the future to acquire a future-self, to fit your ideas and life purpose.

These two exercises and the result will be the basis upon which you can design and build your entire new framework of life possibilities. I am sure that there are other techniques or teachings to undo death wishes which I am not aware of. Normally, I hold these workshop two to three times a year. For information and workshops, see my website at www.physicalimmortality.net. It is important to do clearing, whether or not you have the opportunity to do my workshop.

The following areas of focus (in no specific order) include personal/physical issues that are necessary to address and internally master, according to one's individual situation. Each area of focus is considered a marker of the progress and a constituent of being in the process of physical immortality. They include:

- exchange of fear and misery with love and inner power;
- respect for and appreciation of your physical body;
- exercise—yoga, breathing, hopping on rebounder;
- somatic therapies—correct structural limitation;
- body conditioning (tone, flexibility and elasticity);
- body-system cleansing—liver, colon, parasites, pH balance, rid mouth of all mercury;
- synchronization of the brain with bodily organs;
- control and enhancement of energy flow;
- immune system modification;
- body-mind communication (balanced automatic system);
- all levels of consciousness in sync;
- new beliefs creating new organs;

- physical change on a cellular level;
- confidence in physical image;
- adjustment of body structure and viscera;
- use of all senses in internal communication;
- ability to see a greater view and the significance of an entire event at the time it occurs;
- ability to modify behavior in order to achieve a different outcome instantaneously;
- no judgment of self or fellow human beings;
- the use of love, understanding, and empathy in human exchange;
- distinguishing between observation, the description of events and judgment;
- love as the primary motivator in human exchange;
- wholeness—self-love, physical purification, fearlessness, and confidence;
- self-assurance, power, and kindness as tools for communication;
- the presence of joy at all times —a singing heart;
- the ability to wake up every morning with a smile in your heart—being "alive";
- nutrition (food) modification, instinctively and at your own pace; and
- breatharian "living on light"—personal choice.

LAPI
Walking On The Path

Commitment to life

Self love

Focus on life

Inner intimacy

Optimal health

Oneness

Wholeness

Figure 12: LAPI Walking on The Path

This transformational work can be achieved very simply and can be helped by outside work in therapies and educational practices. There is no need to be concerned about not reaching all of the markers as fast as your mind wants it to happen. The levels must be achieved at one's own pace. Some goals will be acquired more quickly than others.

Patience is a virtue, procrastination is a flaw. You may experience dynamic changes happening to you in as early as a few weeks. This basic transformation is the groundbreaking that leads to a path of enlightenment. It is important to remember that whether you are attempting physical immortality, or you wish to remain mortal and engage in the process just to accomplish the listed markers, it will enhance the quality of your life. In fact, once you experience the feeling of joy and love from within different areas of your body, and a physical manifestation of change is occurring, this will cause you to want more change to be realized throughout the rest of the body.

One major objective of this writing I mentioned earlier, is to help you to recognize your own ability to reach a vision of yourself and your surroundings from a higher point than society dictates for you. We all have vision, the difference between a person who can envision a future and one who cannot, is the distance, depth and clarity of their perception and their ability to consider new possibilities.

Learning to form new visions, new outcomes, new beliefs, stopping aging, renewing body organs, and creating new self-awareness is the learning program I offer in this book.

Create your own program, and remember, self-discovery and renewal can take as much time as needed. There are no comparisons by which to judge the wondrous unfolding and introduction of yourself to YOU!

More LAPI advantages
There are many advantages to being in the process of physical immortality. Eternal life is beautiful and body mastery is virtuous. The primary advantage of this way of being is the quality of life that comes with the

new beliefs. From all, one outcome that stands out is the health issue. In LAPI the individual will have a major advantage over the ordinary mortal person. The way the immune system is reprogrammed, there is no place for disease to flourish or exist. The immune system is reprogrammed to function in a different mode, without restriction as imposed by other parts of the body. Without fear of the death syndrome anymore, and once you have changed your beliefs about death, you have relieved your body from the deepest self-imposed curse ever. Once this occurs, one must also maintain their inner terrain, or pH in state of balance. This is a very important condition for the physical body to sustain. When the body is acidic, it negatively affects all systems in the body. Disease develops and manifests mostly in an acidic bio-terrain (see Chapter 11).

In LAPI, aging is not an issue any longer. Your body can, and will, with the proper direction, halt aging, and in most instances, reverse the aging process. There is no limitation or restriction on the body's ability to rejuvenate itself to the level desired.

Because of our ability to think and communicate within ourselves and with ourselves, it is only a matter of directing the right tunes for the body to respond to in the manner that is desired.

Imagine yourself without the burden of the need to pretend and to judge other humans. Your life becomes simpler to comprehend. The body is clear of the surrounding negative environmental energy and the outpouring of bad news from society. Unlimited possibility, living forever, changing your karma indefinitely, and fear of being controlled become a non-issue.

Starting—the commitment
Knowing that you will likely outlive every person you know, there is no need to get to any point in a hurry. This understanding will become a reminder of your commitment. Are you ready to begin your life anew from this moment on? If yes, for starters, you will need to read this book

again. There is so much new and raw information in this book that you need time to grasp the specifics.

The following are new conversations and statements, you can learn and use in your daily life:

- I will live forever.
- I will live for a long time to come.
- I will never, ever die.
- Death is not a possibility or an option in my life.
- My body rejects all death beliefs.
- I am the sole owner and operator of my body.
- I am responsible for my body's well-being.
- I am in control of my future.

The commitment to your life is important. I am repeating and saying this again in order to emphasize the importance of it. This commitment is not like any other that you have ever made, not in magnitude nor in the attainment of your long-reaching goals. You have to understand that making this type of commitment happens once in a lifetime. This is the ultimate of all possible choices you will ever make. You are making a choice that will affect every aspect of your life.

Once you decide to go for it, your life will change forever. Making this choice is not like any other type of choice you have made in the past. With this choice you are deciding whether you are going to be alive and healthy and freeing your soul, or whether you are eventually going to die and be miserable and get sick while doing so. Once you are part of the process you cannot go back, unless you choose death and want to go back to the death culture like your everyone around you.

When you make the choice and the commitment in your life to be "alive" forever, you are removing yourself from the death energy of the culture that prevails around you. Now you can operate in the culture as

LAPI Achievement

Experiencing a great & healthy life like never before

Loving ourselves & the world in which we live

Helping other humans to extinguish their misery & pain

Raising the human consciousness

Creating a new world for ourselves & others

Reaching to a higher level of communication with the creator

Figure 13: LAPI Achievement

an independent operator, using the technology and all the current advancements to your advantage. This removal of self out of the stormy, miserable, negative environment will leave you inside a clearing space of sorts, where you can repel the noise, the sound and the views of the concentration of death-oriented news and events.

Going to this space is an important step, but you need to be careful not to slip back or to be sucked into the culture of death energy. Becoming an operator in the sense of self-preservation and for the control over your identity is essential in the process of LAPI.

At the same time, just because you are thinking different, feeling different, seeing a truer picture of your culture, that does not give you the right to judge other people and look down at them for not seeing, believing and behaving as you do. It is easy to fall into this trap, which will quickly become destructive. I have experienced this exact process where I was very short tempered and dismissed others for living as mediocre participants in their lives. It is an art to distinguish between observation and crude judgment. When that happens, you need to look inside and ask yourself to find out what you are achieving with this type of expression, especially when you've walked in those very shoes. See but do not judge. With this comes a realization that you are sharpening your visions and your observation skills. It can be a dramatic shift to suddenly have the heightened awareness and acute clarity in observing what goes on around you. If occasions arise that give expression to anger, you can quickly choose to reframe your perspective to one of understanding.

Remember that the goal to achieve in this process is conditioning your physical body to be resilient and vital against all odds. The physical body and all the components which comprise it—your mind, your spirit, your soul, your energy, and all levels of consciousnesses, knows that the goal is sustaining the body. All the above components are linked and meshed together to bring one unified person, they operate in systems like a galaxy functions, energized by one common element of constant energy flow, and together they add up to the sum of one.

They all work in synchronicity between their separate designations and job requirements.

Creating new worlds

With this process, there are many layers of planning and design that may be created in different states, times and space. It's about designing your current world, future world, and inner world. Individual change begins to happen within the initial transformational period. From the time you start putting together your new life, step by step, your body begins to participate as a partner in your new endeavor. This work is to organize your inner world, organize your new life and practice it in a new environment which you are creating. It may take a long time to establish the basis upon which to build a new structure for your world. But when you do, it is important to have all questions asked and answered before the next step (see questions in Chapter 6).

The process of questioning and answering is long and must be satisfying in order to choose new beliefs. Once the basic questions are answered, the process begins to shape the body in cycles of evolvement and to re-invent new body properties. Creating a new world in our mind to begin with, is an incredible process and very rewarding. It is a marvel of a challenge when doing so—you will be able to observe the present world that you are operating within at the very same time as you concentrate on the new world that is taking shape and form. Visualizing a new world never ceases to amaze one, since everyday it evolves within the unlimited space that is now actually available. This formation is a great thrill for the ego. Personal growth will continue to be developed by leaps and bounds. Inner power is accumulated in the form of confidence and self-acknowledgment.

The next step is a place where you will be reconciling your needs with the world around you. From your point of view, you may notice others around you are in a stalemate position, similar to a car placed in neutral. They are not directing or conducting their lives—they have given up their power to do so. One major shift in personal development is the change in our perception of the surrounding world. Noticing the black and white pictures of the culture of death causes you to be more responsive to the plight of the sufferers in your surroundings. You have to live physically in this world, and, for the time being, you need to readjust your new approach to the environment which you are accustomed to operating within.

The former environment that you are familiar with can be a depressing and negative one, where you still have close relatives and friends. In the beginning there is a dilemma concerning such relationships. How best to handle this situation? How to approach a solution to the disparity between where you are and what you see around you? And what consideration is to be given to account for and explain the changes you have made in your life?

One thing for certain, do not feel reservation to talk about your new views. Your views belong to you. It really does not matter if your friends and relatives understand, accept, or ridicule you. The important thing is that you have expressed your feelings and stated your mind. Do not expect sympathy or understanding. This new belief system, ideas and behaviors are, at best, threatening to the beliefs that make up most people's lives. Since you will be in the minority, do not expect many mortals' endorsement of your outrageous ideas. Always remember that in the world of the unlimited, each individual chooses his life and his beliefs, and you need to respect the wishes of other humans.

From my experiences in this stage of relationships, I find many that expect me to fade out with my stands, and revert to the norm. For some I become an interesting conversation at dinnertime. Having chosen to be at this juncture, steadfast to my new beliefs, can be looked at as a revolutionary and unpatriotic gesture to the listener. To my advantage, because of my lively physical body and the strong piercing energies I run most of the time, which seems to evoke further fear and polarization about me and my intentions, there is no neutrality found there. To have a one on one relationship, the parameters are clearer, however, it is not easy to find a match in all aspects of living.

Enjoying the Process of LAPI

Operating in the sea of love

Utilizing withheld creativity

Creating a new action field

Producing unlimited possibilities

Identifying with new beliefs

Experiencing & becoming your own beliefs

Figure 14: Enjoying the Process of LAPI

Ageless Living, Freedom From The Culture of Death

If I can give one piece of advice regarding finding and choosing a mate, it is to be certain that the person you consider becoming your lover, mate love themselves more than anything else (more than their pet and the food they eat!). This person needs to be connected to their inner-child 100%. When you find this person, it will be like receiving a great gift. It will be worthwhile and rewarding to work on and nurture a relationship. If these ingredients are missing, then there is a difficult experience ahead of you.

Most of the people around you will eventually die, and you will be on your own, but there will always be people who we surround ourselves with, and family we create its our choice. You need to understand that death is a choice, and each individual normally makes this choice according to the culture of death's requirement.

If you find yourself in this position, becoming a loner is not a bad thing to be. In the mortal view, a loner has a negative connotation, which is attributed to pretending and social judgments. For an immortal, being alone is okay. You have your inner power at your disposal, so there is no loneliness in your life even if you are alone. For one thing, you have your inner child with you all the time.

Here I emphasize again an important issue that will come up frequently as you embark on your process, which is the need to differentiate between describing an observation and having a judgment on observation. The latter is not an acceptable option. Sometimes it is best to clarify yourself explicitly to avoid misunderstandings of your position. Do not panic if you have a hard time with judgementalism at some point, I did too, and it is a temporary state where you distinguish yourself from the ignorance of others. Remember, mortal people get offended easily by judgments. On the other hand, you know that you are going to live forever, and you have no need to fear any situation or event in your life. At the same time, judgments from others are meaningless and entertaining at best. Nothing is going to happen to you regardless of any judgmental circumstances that may occur.

During this process, you will be working on many different aspects, such as building your character, recreating your goals, your dreams and all the possibilities of the immortal person that you are transforming into. This is a slow process of concentration and cannot be hurried or cut short. Being in the process creates such a powerful awareness that you are keenly alert to the changes taking place. You may sprinkle drops of joy on those in your environment, who are living in the death culture—now a learning ground for you, which can help you define your life. Motivation to focus on your new-found life will be increased. Remember, it is hard to break through the fears and objections that are part of this culture. Do not expect to have an easy time making your transformation in the presence of others. You don't have to justify your position to anyone—you are simply leading and showing the way.

Once you develop this mode of operation and being in the world, all the compassion and the love that you can give to others will be your standard mode of function. Of course, you become a very successful person by virtue of your need to live a long life. Planning for your retirement is absurd and degrading. Only dead and dying people need to "protect" their families with life insurance. The immortal person can produce as much money as he or she needs whenever it is needed. There is no retirement in your future because you are not getting old, sick or debilitated. Success is a certainty in your future. It will be up to you when to reach this place of pure choice. All negative thoughts that normally run in your mind will dwindle and then completely disappear. Your mind will operate on positive thoughts resulting in positive realities and outcomes. In learning to be the creator of your world as well as an example for others, you will use only positive imaging, positive responses and positive techniques.

Persistency
Being in the process of LAPI will definitely change your life for the better, and within a short time you will know and feel the excitement of being truly alive. This is an important reminder for you, the practitioner. As we are human with all the background of behavioral traits that we managed to collect throughout our lives, there is one specific act of

behavior that always seems to reoccur in our lives and may persist in LAPI. That is the human mental ability to convince its own physical being not to continue on a chosen path, or in other words, to talk ourselves out of the commitment and end too early a personal promise to practice certain tasks for improving well-being.

This above challenge is the norm in most cases. I would like to explore this issue and the reasons behind it. It is usually the case that as soon as a person starts to feel improvement and positive changes happening in his/her life while following a specific direction or treatment, something strange happens. The mind starts the process of forgetting the commitment and cuts short the length of the proposed treatment or practice, thinking that the body-mind is doing okay and there is no need for further improvement, almost as if it cannot improve any further. And for the following period, the body does feel good. However, when the next hurdle appears, all "hell" breaks loose, and again all the problems start to exist. For example, when doing a parasite cleanse, most individuals slack off and will not totally complete the process, letting the eggs and the newly born microbes and worms be fed and nursed again to life. Another example—a ten day antibiotic prescription is rarely followed and completed to the end. As soon as the person starts to feel better and physically improve, he will stop taking the remainder of the pills. This behavior is the most common conduct with individuals regardless of the society or culture. There has not been any emphasis on completing tasks, In the way we are taught to be "functional human beings".

When in LAPI, you need to continue to program yourself everyday, without exception, knowing fully at all times that you are greatly improving your well-being. You will begin to feel the improvement is going to last forever because you can count on the body to know better. It is not the body that failed you, but the logical mind's miscalculation of the it's signals and strength of the negative environment. We have a part of us called the skeptic, which needs to be enrolled and converted to support our views and new endeavors, to become an ally to our cause. The skeptic is one of the important players living in our mind. Normally, it has been trained to protect us from becoming victimized in the culture of death. As mentioned earlier, it is important to solidify all the parts that play roles in our mind's world, to work and support the new beliefs and the new practices we have adapted on our path to immortality.

LAPI
The Process

Utilizing all fields in social advancements

Participating fully in the culture & knowing its limitations

Using technology & science to improve life conditions

Involvement in blaming government & politics is not recommended

Preserving the integrity of your body

Realizing that volunteering your life is not heroism

Promoting & cherishing the physical body

Knowing "safeguards" for the preservation of your body

Accepting all of your attributes: mental, structural, biological, spiritual, energy

Figure 15: LAPI The Process

Chapter 11

Body Detoxification

Cellular communication

Physical immortality is a process one can experience and live, yet not achieve. When in LAPI (the process of becoming physically immortal), one is in the process of achieving greater and greater health and more sound and autonomous mental functioning—as one keeps getting better and better as he or she works on new issues and advances in his or her humanity. Being in the process is the greatest thing a person can experience, however it does take work and a personal commitment to oneself. You always need to be vigilant in keeping your guard up, and be acutely aware of the self-serving temptations and mass hypnosis that power elements in society. Remember, commitment and personal will are the two most important requirements for one to make a successful journey into a new and fulfilling realm of life.

The words "physical immortality" are the only words I recommend using which can describe the meaning of seeking to live forever in a physical body. These words are symbolic with vibration and frequency and speak directly and powerfully to the cells of the body. In this way the message is received with clarity and elementary simplicity. The cells must be made certain of their potential and your wishes, and they will act accordingly. It is also important to use precise and definitive words when envisioning your goals for health and absolute fitness, in order for the subconscious to understand and get the message clearly, without ambiguity. The message must be direct and straightforward, with only one meaning to it. The body is listening to the conversation, and specifically to the statements that you say out loud or in thought, regarding the conditions of your life. Again, neither the body nor the subconscious is capable of appraising, translating or distinguishing the input it processes. In other words, directives from you are literally translated. Therefore, using the words/concept "physical immortality", or others as exact, tells our body at the cellular level that it is safe and it is expected to provide life endlessly. For example, if you say, "I want to live my life to age 90 or 170", the standard of time is not a discernible distinction. By virtue of agreeing to die in the future, the immune system begins to facilitate death in the body. Using the words "physical immortality" removes any ambiguity and speaks to the cells both directly and subconsciously.

Regarding the concept of physical immortality, the length and quality of one's life is determined by the beliefs and the messages that have entered the subconscious through various paths and actions, and by the level of life-force that the body has, which maintains functionality as a viable being. Repetition of new programming and reflective suggestions to the self that honor the self are very important techniques that reach the subconscious, and thus every cell of the body

Power of influence
The power of influence from others, whether solicited or unsolicited, is an obstacle to one's own individual creative thinking and becomes mental and energetic toxicity when accepted as truth. Making no decision to be your own lawmaker, you become a receiver of all things, ultimately leading to a total sense of confusion. When you receive something into your thoughts, be it good, bad or indifferent, you do so by your own choosing and allowance, either deliberately or by default. Here is where selective filtering is crucial. Selective filtering is the ability to discern what you wish to accept and what you wish to reject, and that which will empower and stimulate you. You will no longer view yourself as, or feel a lesser human. You will no longer feel flustered, overwhelmed, worried or confused.

Body cleansing & purification
Cleansing and detoxification are normal functions of the body. We have specific systems to get rid of unwanted material and toxins in the body. Further, one can use techniques and methods of cleansing which have

stimulus agents in them to help remove toxic material. Because of the denatured cooked food that we eat which does not contain enzymes and has no life force, we carry mucus, toxins, pathogens and congestion in the intestines and body. The main cause is known as hardened mucoid fecal matter, and is the reason for many diseases.

There are many cleansing methods and techniques from many sources that all have the right idea in principle. Yet, most are only a temporary patch to a very sad affair—the deteriorating condition of our bodies. I have personally tried many of them, getting marginal results with most. Fasting is one good method to help rid the body of toxins for a time. Of course, a change in lifestyle is called for to maintain a healthy and clean inner terrain.

There are specific therapies to help detoxify the different systems, including:

- fasting;
- water fasting;
- special diets;
- colon therapy, enemas;
- herbal therapy;
- lymphatic drainage therapy; and
- specific organ cleansing tinctures, homeopathic.

For more information on suggested cleansing, see my website at: ***www.energeticbalancing.us***

Parasite contamination
Food is the number one reason for the body's aging process. It is a poison to the system, thwarting the ability of the body to operate at optimum condition and bringing it to a minimal basic function. There is a hierarchy of food types and ways of eating. When living in a culture of death, food is the king and ruler of all addictions. Food is the single

most powerful addiction that is dumbing our culture. Our belief in and need to consume food "to stay alive" is deeply entrenched inside of us. One of the main problems that arises from eating food is that the food we eat is being shared with parasites inside of us. Parasitic problems in humans create a "symbiotic" relationship with this lower form of life inside our organs and these parasites persist because we are feeding them.

We contract parasites in a number of ways, and they remain there because we feed them with our bad habits. They become accustomed to our way of life—drinking alcohol; eating and craving sweets and carbohydrates; taking medicines and vitamins; and eating all types of food. They become so addicted to food and smell, that they have their own cravings and addiction to food. They happily feed off of what we ingest and demand more, thus creating our own internal craving for more of these toxins. This relationship with bacteria, worms, fungus and virus is totally needless and destructive to the entire body. These suckers of energy drain the body on all levels of activity. When the body becomes host to parasites, the body loses the integrity of the digestive system, and sooner or later, other major organ systems start to dysfunction.

Parasites thrive in a acidic, imbalanced and fermented environment. They live and flourish in groups and most have their own territory and do not mingle with other species or types. Parasites, fungus and bacteria thrive in, and are immune to toxicity in the body. They can mutate and create a new breed of microbe, making themselves all the more resilient. It is ironic that the body is decaying but the parasites are flourishing. In our culture we allow this to happen through diet, pets in the home and victim attitudes.

Most people are good hosts to parasites and lack the awareness of their existence, or the knowledge of how to clear them. In my opinion, this is the most disgusting, decaying energy we can carry around with us and sleep with. Individuals that are hosts most likely have a contractual agreement with the various parasites inside them. It is difficult to cleanse/clear out the parasite unless the agreement is voided or broken in advance. Parasite hosts carry with them the negative energies of decay and influence the energetic matrix of other individuals around them who they come into contact with. Each parasite has its' own frequency and during infestation, the carrier host can live and behave in a parasitic mode of action.

It is very important to clear parasites out of our energetic and physical matrix—it is not ok to be a host, it will lower the entire vibration of the body. There is not enough awareness in the medical world to eliminate parasites. They try only to kill the pathogen, not remedy the cause. One must change their internal environment and pH balance through diet and cleansing, not just take a pill to kill the creature. The best method I have found which works well to control parasites is to starve them to extinction. For persons living on light, parasites will not be an issue to deal with. The inner terrain of the body will not accommodate parasitic conditions.

Information for parasite cleanses
I provide this information for parasite cleanses on my website—**www.energeticbalancing.us** It is posted for your convenience and it is best to check with your medical adviser for the appropriate cleanse.

Parasites are common, but require your commitment and tenacity to clear them from the body. They thrive in an acidic environment and feed on what you ingest, creating a host of imbalances and cravings. Parasites and yeasts are like Siamese twins and are always seen together. It is important to begin an anti-yeast nutritional program while you do a parasite cleanse, to prevent you from generating new toxins in the body. This means elimination of wheat, sugar (including fruit), dairy, meat and processed products. A diet of predominantly vegetables and small amounts of whole grains (excluding wheat) is recommended.

It is important that you achieve 2-3 bowel movements before beginning a parasite cleanse. If not you will need to find a good colon cleanser before or during the program. Some products have what's needed to sweep the colon in their program. These are noted. Colonics and enemas are also recommended.

These programs all differ in duration. It is generally understood that to kill yeasts, parasites, their eggs & larvae requires 60 days or longer. Below I provide helpful information in finding a program for eliminating parasites. Take a look, do your own research and choose one that is right for you. Clearing the body of parasites and yeasts is a journey which will result in overall improvement in your physical and mental functioning and will probably change your life. Stick with it, you're worth it.

These products can be obtained at health food stores or on-line when indicated. Happy cleansing!!

- Pure Body Institute—*"Para-Cleanse"* & *Colon Booster*— call 1-800-952-7873, or go to **www.pbiv.com**

- Dr. J's Detox Products—*"Yeast-Para Control"*—designed for use with *Cleansing-Balance Tea* to clear debris. Click on "Health Maintenance Recommendations" for some good and useful information at **www.drjshealthnet.com**

- Nature's Secret—*"Parastroy"*—has internal sweep with product. Available at health food stores, or go to **www.vitacost.com** for a discounted price

- Renew-Life—*"Para-Gone"*—also purchase *Fiber-Smart* and *Para-Zyme,* they must be used separately for colon & enzyme cleansing—available at health food stores or go to **www.renewlife.com**

- Dr. Natura—*"Colonix"*—intestinal & parasite cleanser all-in-one— **www.drnatura.com**

- Herbal Gardens—*"Inner Purity"*—also recommend using *Inner Clarity* first if you're not having 2-3 bowel movements a day—**www.thelifetree.com**

- Dr. Hulda Clarke's—*"Parasite Cleanse"*—**www.drclarkstore.com** or **www.drclarkia.com** for a very simple, potent tincture

- Gaia Herbs—*Black Walnut/Wormwood tincture*—easy to take drops; available at health food stores or they may have their own brand—should have Black Walnut, Wormwood & Cloves

Chapter 11: Body Detoxification

- Blessed Herbs—*Parasite Elimination Kit*—click on "Cleansing Kits" at **www.blessedherbs.com**

- Arise & Shine—*Parasite Cleanse*—**www.ariseandshine.com**, or contact Carl Barna @ 858-518-6999

These are suggestions and informational only. Always consult your doctor or qualified health care practitioner.

Importance of pH balance

pH balance is the degree to which the body is either acidic or alkaline (base). This means in the blood, saliva, urine and tissues. pH indicates the concentration of hydrogen atoms (positively charged molecules) in any given part of the body. pH is measured on a scale of 1 to 14, 7 being neutral. Below 7 is considered (by most practitioners) acid and above alkaline, with varying opinions on the exact numbers, but that is generally the rule.

Overacidification of the body is a condition which is perfect for sustaining mycroforms (fungus, virus, bacteria, parasites, etc.) and is perpetuated by the standard American diet of processed, sweet, caffeinated, nutritionless foods. Some, such as Dr. Robert Young, believe that it is the factor which underlies all disease.

An alkaline environment is a balanced inner terrain which can be achieved through diet and creating a peaceful state of mind. Basically, a diet rich in fresh vegetables and small amounts of whole grains (wheat free) is a good place to start.

I will not get into a lengthy discussion on the subject, but suffice it to say that it would behoove every human being to look into the benefits of alkalizing the body and how to do that. The charts on the following pages can be helpful in determining what foods are considered acidic or alkaline. I highly recommend reading *"The pH Miracle"*, by Dr. Robert Young.

That said it is good to remember how much emotion and attitude come into play here and that no amount of alkalizing is going to create lasting change if one holds onto old, negative patterns of thought. Ultimately, when one is living in mastery, nutritional value is not always important, but most people need to feed the body in the healthiest way possible to create greater conditions of ease and energy on their path.

Acid forming foods

- alcohol
- all processed foods
- anger
- barley
- birds
- breads—baked or any
- cake
- canned fruits and veggies
- cereals—all
- chickpeas
- chocolate
- cigarettes
- coffee
- complaining
- cooked grains—except millet and quinoa
- corn—dried
- cornstarch
- crackers
- dairy products
- drugs
- eggs
- fish
- foods cooked with oils
- fruits, glazed or sulfured

- ketchup
- legumes
- lentils
- meat
- mustard—prepared
- nuts, seeds, beans
- oatmeal
- pasta
- pepper—black
- popcorn
- salt
- shellfish
- soft drinks
- soy products
- soy beans—fresh
- stress
- sugar, white and processed
- sweeteners, artificial (S*plenda, Equal, Aspartame*, etc.)
- tea, black & green
- tomatoes
- vegetables, overcooked
- vinegar, distilled
- vitamin C
- wheat, all forms

Chapter 11: Body Detoxification

Alkaline forming foods

All fresh and raw fruits, vegetables, and sprouts, including those listed here:

- alfalfa sprouts
- apple cider vinegar
- apples
- appreciation
- apricots
- avocados
- bananas
- barley
- beans—green
- beets & greens
- berries
- blackberries
- broccoli
- brussels sprouts
- cabbage
- cantaloupe
- carrots
- cauliflower
- celery
- cherries
- collard greens
- cucumbers
- dates
- dulse
- figs
- fresh corn
- fresh, raw juice
- fun
- goat whey
- grapefruits
- grapes
- herbal teas
- honey
- kale
- kelp
- leaf lettuce
- leeche nuts
- lemons
- lima beans—green
- limes
- love
- mangoes
- maple syrup
- melons—all
- millet
- molasses
- mushrooms
- mustard
- okra
- onions
- organic olive & flax seed oils
- parsley
- parsnips
- peaches
- pears
- peas, green
- peppers
- pineapple
- plums
- prunes
- quinoa
- radishes
- raisins
- raspberries
- rhubarb
- rutabagas
- sauerkraut
- spinach
- squash
- turnip greens
- watercress
- yams

Chapter 12:

Living on Light & Nutrition

In the beginning
Physical immortality is the return to the source. Humans began their existence as physical immortals and as breatharians. The question is, when was the beginning of humanity as we know it? I believe that our advanced race of human beings is a new species that is hardly connected with earlier humanoids. About ten thousands years ago, visitors from other worlds reprogrammed human's behaviors in the form of new beliefs and created one unified class of mortality. In the story of Adam and Eve, Adam ate the apple and began using his intestinal tract which wasn't in use previously—this is the era where the new earth inhabitancy arrived. Why was eating the apple such a big deal? This act changed a system, which until then, had operated through the body's breathing mechanism, to a system where man needed to gather, prepare, eat, consume, digest, process and eliminate that fruit. In doing so, humans started the transition into food digestion, which began a toxic influence on the body. This transition to a stage of fruitarianism changed the body's energy consumption and output, thus changing the structure and the operation of energy flow and brought in the involvement of the emotions when consuming food. This change caused a less optimal use of energy by allowing the food to introduce the so called "secret of life", in other words, it was the introduction to aging, and ultimately, to death.

At the time of the biblical apple, food was the main reason for the shift from living forever to merely living less than one thousand years. As fire was introduced, other options for cooking and combining different foods together presented themselves. The more poison that was created and consumed, the more it was accepted by the body. When humans became organized under groups by territory, religions brought into their awareness the concept of death, and the fear of it was introduced to humans. At that point, the human body accelerated it's deterioration, and shortened the length of life to less than 100 years. Those two important causes, the consumption of food and the belief in death, will guarantee the death of every human.

Nutrition & well-being

Our culture assumes that food is the only way for nourishing the body and is a source of energy to promote life. We think that food as we know it can be only a positive thing for us. This is a predigested assumption without any solid basis. Food is actually the source for most energy depletion in the body. Food consumption is the main reason we lose energy and functionality most of the time. Regardless of the type of food you prepare for its "nutritional value", whether you are a fast food eater, vegetarian, fruitarian, raw foodist or instinctive eater, after eating you will lose energy. The more a person eats at one sitting, the more biological and energetic systems will shutdown. I consider most foods toxic and an energetic drain.

Partaking in food is a major part of our belief system. The less food you eat, the more energy and better overall existence you will have for longer periods of time. It is important to note here that the entire economy of the world is based on producing food, the primary objective being to feed its inhabitants. By doing so, it is causing the death of the same people it feeds. It is a cycle of death programming and a cycle of beliefs that perpetuate a condition of pain, misery and disease.

Because many societies around the world eat heavy at lunch, they experience system shutdown and must take a siesta because of the energy depletion. Many stop all activity of the body to allow the digestive system to continue the work of processing the food. The personal beliefs in the value of the food and the expectation of nutritional gain, create the tolerance needed within each individual to extend and manage the eating escapade of digestion and elimination. Food can be fun if eaten in the smallest portion possible. You still enjoy the taste, smell and texture of what you ingest, without using all your energy for digestion. For eating individuals, it is very important to remember that the size of the stomach is approximately the size of their fist, so, even one spoon above that size will be detrimental to the flow of energy.

I personally have nothing against food as long as I do not have to digest it. I was addicted to the smell, texture, and taste. Food is a huge commodity in our world—imagine people eating food with preservative chemicals that last longer than its wrapping. When I walk through the aisles in the supermarket (even "health food stores"), I get blown away when looking at all the dead food that is sitting on the shelves, wondering at how resilient the human body is to endure all the hardened and toxic materials that we pay money to put inside our bodies.

My personal experience when receiving food from my mother throughout the years was, and is, that it is nothing but an expression of her love to me. It is de facto non-verbal communication. The symbols of love and food are crossed. Food is not the love that kids require from their mothers.

When I live on pranic nourishment exclusively, and I mention to my mother that I do not eat food, it does not register in her mind at all. She starts laughing and giggling, thinking it is a joke I play and cannot comprehend the idea.

Body wonder
At present on earth, humans are poisoning their bodies more quickly and more dramatically than ever before. The body's capacity to adjust to, assimilate and accommodate new poisons that enter the body system is amazing. For example: if you smoke your very first cigarette today, you probably will react to the smoke by coughing, nausea and a burning sensation in your lungs. You knowingly allowed this toxic air to enter your body, and your body reacted appropriately, signaling to your conscious mind to stop the nonsense, and reject the poison. However, when you try to smoke the next day again for the second time, your body will show less resistance, altering its functions to allow the smoke to enter the lungs, and will adjust to the new situation, accepting the poisonous smoke even though the body knows that the smoke will harm it.

What can be learned from this? First, that the body is a very unique machine that can alter its functions and adapt to a new situations in order to survive and preserve the body's existence in spite of ingestion of poison (slow death). Secondly, that the body responds directly to beliefs and actions. In all situations, when new acquired beliefs and actions are detrimental to well-being, the body will adjust, abiding by the new situation and adhere to the new programming of the new belief, even though symptoms may be present.

What we learn from the behavior of the body is, first, the body can accept poison and carcinogens, adjusting its mechanism to facilitate the acceptance of the poison, and second, the body becomes addicted to the chemicals as a result of the poisons. Of course these body behaviors work on either, positive life supporting beliefs or ones that sabotage the energetic matrix of the body.

With the brilliance of the mechanism of our body, it will continue deteriorating and changing its operation to adapt to the environment and to the lifestyle we hold. It started a long time ago, taking thousands of years to evolve and descend to our current level of being. The life force and vitality levels which I see in my work now average at 53, on a scale of 0-100. Fortunately, reversing this trend is possible, feasible, doable and practical. But it is going to take more than a week's seminar to reverse a life trend! It is a process that will go on forever for each of us. There is basic work to be done, and this work may entail years of practice. The commitment is of the utmost importance to overcoming the negative and limiting influences of the surrounding culture.

Do not expect to jump and hop in the beginning when in LAPI, rushing to act on all of the aspects of a correction list at once will be very confusing. It is better to spread out the program, and take one step at a time, to allow time to be your own lover. Time will become your friend and escort. To hurry time or rush toward achievements is no longer applicable. When in LAPI, you will have all the time you need without limitation, to elevate yourself to the "ELOHIM" (the Gods) world.

Chapter 12: Living on Light & Nutrition

Breatharianism & living on light

Breatharianism or living on light, is a lifestyle characterized among other things, by the absence of eating, resulting from the expanding of the consciousness sphere in which a person lives. Technically, the true practicing breatharian has no need to eat or drink in order to keep the body functioning perfectly. A breatharian consumes no food and no drink.

On Joachim Werdin's website, he describes his experience very plainly. *"Most non-eating people who name themselves breatharians, drink some water, tea, coffee or other beverages from time to time."* Some of them, in order to satisfy the sense of taste, eat a piece of chocolate, a cookie, some cheese, horseradish or something else once in a while. Non-eating individuals have rid themselves of the need for dependency upon food for nutrition, breaking the addiction to the food we have come to believe to be a must to ingest to maintain life. Freeing oneself from the need to eat food, digest and eliminate it, for the sake of accepting this cultural belief system, is a winning choice with lots of benefits.

There is a fundamental difference between quitting food (not eating) and fasting. It is the belief in the need for and the value of food. If you believe you need to eat in order to maintain health, then you must eat to live and survive your own expectations. Breatharians do not believe in and accept food as a means to receive nutrition for maintaining life. Breatharians receive their nutrition and life force strictly from prana, or breath. They are not fasting, they just do not believe in wasting energy on processing food in their bodies. This energy is now reserved for a life centered upon fulfillment from higher sources and the implications of that on many levels. Cosmic energy, whether it is called prana, chi, qi, ki, life-force, vitality level and liquid, light is the main form of nutrition for all living creatures.

A person who drinks liquid food regularly, e.g. juices, can't be called a breatharian. A person who is fasting or on a starvation diet can't be called a breatharian, because the situation is only temporary—food consumption will be resumed and their belief in nutrition remains intact. A person who by force refrains from eating can't be called a breatharian. Such action, if prolonged, is harmful to the body and can lead to death. Fasting and starvation diets are different subject matters altogether.

Breatharianism is a state of being and activism to have total freedom from the need for food, disease, aging and limiting lifestyle. It can also appear as a side effect of expanding one's consciousness sphere. Sometimes, it can happen unexpectedly and can last for a few months or years. A breatharian can choose to eat or not to eat, but one thing is certain, breatharians don't need to eat to keep the body working normally and optimally.

At the beginning of our civilization, there were always people who never ate. Such people existed, exist and will always exist, which means that you too have this capability. It is a return to source and uses the lungs as the main energy receptor and nutrition distributor. We humans can use one or both systems: nourishment from food or pranic nourishment. If you are a food eater, you are using both systems together, whether you know it or not. Eating food is a very inefficient method of nourishment and in most cases the individual gains zero energy from processing the food. The breathing of air and use of prana are the main collectors of cosmic energy that maintain the level of chi and life force to keep the body sustained and vital.

In the book, *"Living on Light"*, one of a number of books written by Jasmuheen, she describes in detail the philosophy, techniques and learning principles of pranic nourishment. She has a most brilliant mind, has an uncanny ability to express herself with eloquence and has great mastery in transmitting thoughts and ideas to a collective group of people. I totally value her contribution to the world, bringing new possibilities, new options and new choices for the masses. Jasmuheen is the one that brought the simple and natural concept of living on light into the forefront of the world, where one can live life in total freedom from the constraints of the culture. I would like to take this opportunity to thank Jas for who she is.

Chapter 12: Living on Light & Nutrition

Breatharianism is the ultimate practice and state of mind that allows one to be in a space of optimal wellness. Starting to learn the secrets of breatharianism is to open the way to the most perfect and deepest understanding about oneself. This is another realm of existence. A state of wholeness and oneness are prerequisites. Clearing of trauma and old beliefs, cleansing all systems of the body (detoxification), and programming new visions and beliefs and acting on them, should be in place and practiced, before any attempt to switch to become Breatharian.

It is clear that if you stop eating food there is already a state of freedom from the old habitual belief that without food you cannot survive and live. It frees the consciousness from the burden of food and frees the energy in you. There is a process in which you will move from a food eating creature to a breathing being, sustained on water only. This process is known as pranic nourishment, see *"Living on Light"* by Jasmuheen. The body will automatically draw the energy from the universal energy source, which is all around you. Once you assimilate this energy directly, there will be no limit to your energy.

The opportunity to not eat for some period of time can be most rewarding, knowing without fear that it is okay. Using a detoxification process period for a month or two at a time can be the right step on the way to breatharianism.

A person who plans to work toward becoming a breatharian needs to be certain that the entire "must-do list" is in practice and that all the markers have been realized. Being in LAPI, by itself, is a state of no limitation and living forever. Many people stay in LAPI while on raw foods and that is okay. I strongly and unequivocally discourage attempting to shift to living on light without proper preparation, and highly recommend consultation with your health advisors and counselors. It is most important to maintain your well-being and safety as the first order in LAPI. Don't defeat your own purposes by engaging in something that is either premature or wrong for you to pursue. Remember, there is no hurry to do anything—you have all the time in the world working for you.

Living on light—my personal experience

Living as physically immortal for the last decade, practicing my inherent instinctive will to live forever in this body, cleansing, detoxifying, deprogramming old parasitic beliefs and conditioning I collected through time, has been the most rewarding undertaking of my life. Living in the realm of mastering my body-mind functions, and experiencing total wholeness in and out of my body most of the time is supreme. For many years I knew all along that eating food was like poisoning my body day in and day out. I personally have moved into clearing outright the second deepest belief all humans harbor in the depths of their being, the belief in food.

For years I tried to minimize my food intake and the type of food I chose at different periods of my life to avoid the inefficiency of processing food in the intestine. I called myself all kinds of names to describe my practices, state of mind, and beliefs—I was vegetarian, vegetarian raw foodist, macrobiotist, raw foodist, instinctive raw foodist, fruitarian, juicing specialist and any combination possible.

The aspects that most confuse the ordinary person who eats food, is the fact that food is equated with love (mother love), and with nutrition. These are accepted beliefs and social promises, which have nothing to do with what is real. So for years and years I discussed and talked about quitting eating food with every person that I got to know. I knew that not eating was safe and sound. However, at first I wanted to meet a person that had the experience of not eating for long periods of time. I researched the subject, called and contacted anyone that knew anything about it. I met Wiley Brooks, read his book and interviewed him at length to find out all I could. He was very interesting and committed energetically to create a better and safer world for us, helping individuals in their quest for longevity. And of course he is into transforming himself.

Later I met some members of the first group to do the 21 day process in Australia with Jasmuheen. Some of the group went on living on light for years. I met Paul and Eva Lowe and others in that group at Harbin

Hot Springs. This was all I needed to see. Then I read Jasmuheen's book *"Living on Light."* It was the most accurate and straightforward book I had ever read. By then, it was only a matter of time—what day do I quit eating? I had prepared myself in every possible way for this moment, expecting to go through all the steps mentioned in the book when doing my 21 day process.

Choosing the moment was important at the time. My heart was singing—the main indicator for readiness. Once I quit eating, I knew that all was perfect—I did not have to be confined during the 21 days. On the 4th day I had to fly to Denver for a week of meetings, a lecture and a workshop. Losing the weight in the first week was not dramatic to me, but for others who knew me, they were very uncomfortable hearing that I quit eating and was shrinking in front of their eyes.

For the next 18 months I was very steadfast and committed to my new way of life. A few times during this period I would go to Whole Foods Store and smell and taste certain flavors. Not eating and the need for food was a none issue. Physically I was fit and in the most optimal weight and shape that I had ever been. The only down side was the social aspect of living and working in mainstream community. As time went on, I was shunned by some people and friends, there were fewer invitations to social gatherings and many were skeptical and felt uncomfortable eating around me. At the year and a half mark I proclaimed to my friend that I no longer lived solely on prana. However, I really never could go back to eating food in any way I had in the past. The nutritional value of the food was no longer a consideration, but the processing of it was. So I began experimenting with different ideas of having food which was easiest to process efficiently. In other words, to eat something that would not suck my energy being processed inside me, and would leave my digestive system the fastest.

Of course, for me taste was and is the only criteria to eating any food. Since I do not care for the nutritional value whatsoever, I, in no way reject any food. All the old beliefs about this food or that food being better than the other are all totally meaningless to me. I never look for the nutritional values, especially with raw food and macrobiotic food—the raw is hard for some to digest and the macrobiotic can be an energy sucker. Looking back at all the lectures I gave to different groups who adhere to specific protocols and telling them about living on light, I realized that there are very few healthy individuals eating these different diets, without exception. Your belief systems and attitudes, which influence the metabolic processes, are the greatest influence on the outcome of eating.

Strictly based upon my opinion and my experience, I've compiled a list of foods that should never be eaten by any human or living creature, as they may eventually cause your demise.

The following list of food items jump out as the most poisonous and toxic to your health, or is an energy sucker:

- any food that is packaged in plastic, cellophane or in a can is a dead food you need to avoid;
- potatoes;
- tomatoes;
- nightshades & fungus;
- carrots and apples—due to the time and energy it takes to process—apple and carrot juice is good;
- oranges & orange juice—too acidic;
- bread, pasta and white rice;
- garlic & salt;
- sweets & sugar substitutes; and
- soybeans, soy drinks, tofu or any soy product.

Bread, pasta and rice have no beneficial nutrients and will stick in your intestines longer than any other food and therefore the body will lose energy for sure. Actually this food will block your energy flow within a few minutes after eating. There is no good reason to eat this food ever.

Chapter 12: Living on Light & Nutrition

Salt, sweeteners and their substitutes are the number one aging agents in the body. Soybeans and soy products are very harmful to the pH level and extremely difficult to digest. They specifically affect hormonal production and are now being shown to cause dysfunctions.

I do not want to ruin your lunch and dinner ideas, but here is something to consider. The best way to consume food is if you can liquefy it and drink it, that way it will move the fastest in your digestive tract, and will do less harm to the energy flow. Never eat at one meal a total amount of food larger than your fist. For measurement, fit all the food inside a "one cup" measuring cup. Any time you exceed this amount you will lose energy. Lastly, eat less. Eat only half what you would normally eat and only when you are truly hungry.

I have been living on light off and on for the past 5 years. I am now back to just drinking water again after returning from a Dark Room Workshop in Thailand. For me not eating food is not the point—not processing food in the intestines is one reason, but the primary reason is knowing that I do not need to eat. I like the way I feel in body and consciousness when my energies are freed up from processing food. I know what works for me, which type of substance to accept and which ones to reject out of hand. Living as a breatharian or just living on light is not an objective for me any longer. I do it as a practical matter, it falls in the category of deprogramming addiction. Physical immortality is the goal and the vision. Living on light can be a starting point to clear old beliefs and behaviors, however by itself living on light does not make you immortal if you are still living in the culture of death, entertaining beliefs and ideas of reincarnation. For some, spirituality and transcending the physical become more important, instead of loving and honoring the physical body, and using it as a tool in accomplishing their highest aspirations. For me not eating is at the same level as shaving my head. Same amount of preparation. On the other hand living as physically immortal is a entire other level and layer of existence.

Chapter 13:

The Joy of Relationships

Got intimacy?
Intimacy with sovereign individuals is totally different from intimacy with dying persons. If you are alive and vibrant, have cleared all death wishes and urges, then you will be totally intimate with yourself. Intimacy exists in a state of wholeness. In this state of being, where self love is the basis of all there is in life, consciously merging all the parts of our body will result in operating harmoniously. Intimacy for me is more of a total self love and appreciation for myself and the ability to manifest my world and my dreams, as the world turns. I cannot be intimate with any person more than that person is intimate with himself. The same goes with expressions of love. Wanting and experiencing intimacy always starts inside. There is no in-between intimacy. When there is only a perception of intimacy, usually based on our cultural standards, as in marriage, this is not necessarily true intimacy. One cannot truly engage with and reciprocate to the flow of energy of another person without true intimacy.

One of the most striking moments in my life was a time when I had to look at myself and evaluate my own level of intimacy. I was doing a written exercise at the time, to investigate the level of my knowledge of who I am. I was blown away as I realized that I knew so little about me. I was a stranger to myself, and had no clue about any basic understanding of myself. I felt no validity to my existence, even though I thought that I knew myself very well without a doubt. At this point I took it upon myself to investigate and find out what and who I am. The mirror on the wall had broken—my perception of my image was no longer acceptable. I found a void that I could not bridge by masking and taping the broken parts. This was a wakeup call that on one hand shattered my world and on the other opened a new door. At that point I realized that if I don't know me, then who will? The answer came very quickly…nobody. That moment became a window, opening the boundaries of my box.

There is an outstanding saying: "Men of quality are not threatened by women of equality". This really sums up the level of harmony which is possible in a good relationship. It is easier to relate to someone who trusts and loves himself in totality, than to have a relationship with a grappling partner who experiences victimization, self doubt, uncertainty and low self-esteem, especially when they are trying to fix humanity!

When you live as physically immortal or are living on light, the body vibration pulses at a higher level and becomes energetically in tune and more sensitive to others in your field. For this reason, sometimes my sensitivity may cause me to temporarily reject energies which are not aligned with me. In other words, we don't always need to relate to everyone around us.

Intimacy & sex

Intimacy, for me, refers to a human ability and feeling that can be queried and understood with such basic questions as: "What is the most tender and hidden aspect about yourself?"; "Do you really know yourself?"; "Do you really love yourself?"; "Are you intimate with yourself?"; "Do you know what personal intimacy is?"

Knowing oneself is the six million dollar answer. When you ask someone "Do you love yourself?" or "…know yourself?", the answer is usually "of course". It sounds fundamental—however, most people confuse their behavioral responses (such as likes and dislikes) with self-knowledge. Intimacy starts deep inside the body. All outside appearances or manifestations of intimacy directly relate to the level of intimacy one has within his own body-mind. In other words, the self-intimacy of the human supersedes and controls all other intimate relationships. As one learns to become intimate with oneself, it is necessary to know and love you the person. Personal intimacy is a fundamental resource in becoming physically immortal. The self-love of all of you is a precondition and the only authentic way to achieve intimacy. Total self-love is intimacy in action. Once that happens, you can extend yourself to others to become intimate with you.

Unfortunately, in this society of death, one of the most important aspects of our definition of intimacy is based on one's ability for sexual performance. We value, measure and rate our life's stability and joy through the ability to perform sexual acts, or any function related to sex, whether they are with a single partner in marriage or not. Sexuality, per se, has nothing to do with intimacy. The level of intimacy that I am referring to is a most basic one. There are a myriad of functions of physical activity in relationships that may be referred to as intimacy, but it is only by name, and not by content. True intimacy extends far beyond the physical, and intimacy is not limited to just one primary individual in our lives, it applies to all of our relationships. When one becomes intimate with himself, he will have no fears and can engage fully, deeply and honestly with other human beings.

In this culture, intimacy is greatly viewed with colored spectacles which are layered with sexual symbolism. Looking through the glasses, one can distinguish and value people only as sexual entities and objects. As a sexual being anything that is not related to sex is not part of his path or part of his future. The view through these glasses is a greatly accepted view of the world. This type of dysfunctional behavior is the outcome of trends and value-setting found, learned, imitated and promoted by the culture. Sex overshadows intimacy by using myths about manhood, pleasure and orgasmic potency of both genders. It is the underlying rationale of trendsetters such as industries who profit from the sexual programming that we are bombarded with. When wearing these glasses and one views the world in this way then all humans turn into living and breathing sexual objects. And their value is only as good as their ability to deliver satisfactory sexual performance, their portrayal of sexuality or sexy appearance.

In the mortal realm and the alpha male world, sex is often viewed as the only indicator and barometer of being alive. This part of the culture elevates sex to be the only true test that humans have at their disposal to validate their existence. Other functions and attributes, such as breathing, thinking, walking, or quality of person, inner beauty, etc. are given lesser value. During a disastrous or life-threatening event, some will envision the act of sex as the last meaningful act of his existence. Sex is expressed as the choice for the last significant action of life. This happens in the mortal world, where death is the ruler and director of human vision, where it is very difficult to see the bigger picture, the future and full cycle of one's life.

In this narrow world vision, there is no future, no possibility, no fun and no joy. It is all about expectation and appearance, from misguided myths, beliefs and programs. The individual who sees the world in this way is looking from within parameters with the rest of society.

In the realm of physical immortality, feeling alive, is constantly present and resonates all the time. The act of intercourse is just a function an individual can perform. When having joy and fun in your life all of the time, the "performance" stigma related to sex is eliminated. Sex becomes a function of joy and fun, and is not limited by any restriction whatsoever. Sex and sexual performance become a beautiful recreation that can also possesses a procreation function. And for some, it is a spiritually enlightened event, and a tool to access greater consciousness.

A "no limitation" setting for those living as immortal suggests, directly and indirectly, that any and all options and possibilities are feasible and acceptable concerning sexual play. There is nothing that an individual cannot do or experience sexually with a consenting partner. All, and any combination of, options and possibilities, are acceptable and permitted as long as no person suffers or is infringed upon. Here it is not being suggested that everybody must engage in every sexual option, however, an individual truly has the right to choose to experience any and all possibilities without limitation. This is true for any type of activity that the individual may elect to engage in, so long as harm is inflicted upon no one and no thing.

Chapter 13: The Joy of Relationships

In this culture, a man is only a man when his penis is hard and he is able to ejaculate. This is a common myth in most societies. Most men connect orgasmic pleasure with ejaculation. In regard to this, ejaculation becomes both a primal goal and, in a sense, somewhat a loss of self. Deep anxiety has plagued men since ancient times over the loss of semen. The ancient Greeks were aware of its intrinsic value. Hippocrates called it "precious", Pythagoras called it "the flower of the blood", and other ancients held that an ounce of semen was worth approximately 40 ounces of blood.

It is a common understanding that all sexual encounters normally end up with ejaculation and a climax. That understanding is the result of mortal conditioning. In the immortality process, the notion that "I must have an ejaculation and orgasmic climax" is not necessarily part of the script, and in most cases is not a direct outcome of sexual activity. Releasing the need for any requirements allows the body and the mind to relax and be present to the real aspect of love-making and intimacy without a pre-planned expectation.

In Taoist texts, erotic expressions are often conveyed through dialogues between the emperor and his Tao love advisors. Here is a Taoist quote: "When a man loves once without losing his semen, he will strengthen his body. If he loves twice without losing it, his hearing and vision will be more acute. If three times, all disease may disappear. If four times, his heart and blood circulation will be revitalized. If six times, his loins will become strong. If seven times, his skin may become smooth. If nine times, he will reach longevity. If ten times, he will be as an immortal." (Change, 1977) I think this is another cultural exaggeration, but can convey the benefit of recirculating the energies. This can apply to the female orgasmic response as much as it does to men.

Tantric techniques and methods of sexual activity are highly recommended. The study of sacred sex will enhance the understanding of the Tantric philosophy and practices, and it can be a great addition to acknowledge the possibilities of human sexual intercourse, as well as provoke an eye-opening response for most Americans. It should be mentioned that at the beginning of your process, the issue of sexuality will be down toward the bottom of the list of what is necessary to master to continue in the process. The more mastery you achieve, the more masterful lover you will become. Being patient, practicing and moving forward in other arenas will be where your strengths and achievements lie. I suggest that everyone take Tantra workshops and learn new ways to look at sexuality and sexual behaviors. The world queen of Tantric teachings is Margot Anand. She conducts workshops around the world. I highly recommend her work. Conscious breathing is constantly employed in her workshops, where she shows how to use it while making love to enhance the duration and intensity of one's pleasure.

When practicing immortality, the issue of sex is a matter of choice and preference, and does not have any influence upon one's ability to live as an ageless being. In this vein, gender preference and orientation are not considered limitations. As with all behaviors and responses, the individual will consciously practice his own beliefs, wishes and desires. There is no right or wrong with regard to making a decision based on any aspect of lifestyle when expansion and growth are the focus.

There is one thing to be cautioned about—make sure not to mingle your bodily fluids with someone you are not sure about or have doubt about the energetic resonance of their body. Your bodily fluid contains all your DNA markings that are active whether inside or outside of you. If it is mixed or deposited into a negative environment, you can become imbalanced for a time. It will be good practice, to make a choice not to engage with any individual with disharmonious energies and stick by it. Even though, when you are in LAPI, you can transmute the negative energy, why do it to begin with. (Along these lines, when having your hair cut or clipping your nails, make sure all the cut pieces are collected and put down the drain, where they will decompose in liquid as soon as possible. That way, you do not deposit your DNA markings in garbage energy, to be energetically mixed there for a long period of time.)

We all share the pleasure of being part male and part female, and possess the androgynous characteristics that comprise the natural aspects of humanity. Nature has produced this condition, perhaps as a way to show us that we need not discriminate against or judge heterosexuals, bisexuals, homosexuals or the asexual, these are irrelevant distinctions.

The Perfect Relationship
by John Kuzich, 1990

The perfect relationship does exist, and it is not to be found in another person, as most of us would have sought to find it. The perfect relationship exists within ourselves, and herein lays the exhilarating reality of the true experience of love and joy. To experience love in a meaningful and lasting way, you must first draw it forth within yourself, in order to establish the foundation that will enable you to give and receive love. The possibilities for love and the relationship of your dreams are endless, but you must first create this relationship internally. You are your dream come true, the perfect mate, and the experience of a lifetime.

Chapter 14:

On the Path

Love without limitation

Love is the most important feeling, experience and expression that any human being can generate. Physical immortality is based on and defined by the love that an individual can shower upon himself and others. The love that physical immortality produces is a kind of love that exhibits eternal patience, infinite mercy and forgiveness. The first recipient of this love must be the self. It is the seed that grows into the tree that produces the fruit—it is the basis of the tree of life. Nothing and no one is really loved unless self-love is secured. Self-love is central to knowing yourself and communicating with your body-mind. When you love yourself, you will take care of all of you, all of the body elemental, without any distinction or separation.

Learning to love is a form of acknowledgement of the body. The manifestation of life that is experienced in it, is at the very least, worth recognition. To love yourself means that you will love all of the parts that constitute the biological you, without exception. You cannot love only what you interpret as the "good" parts of your body, or the parts that you think are more important or attractive than others. Self-love extends even to loving your own disease without discrimination, when disease is present.

As said earlier, all disease is the creation and the manifestation of our own design and manufacture. With illness, one of the biggest and gravest mistakes an individual can make is to dislike his own disease and treat it as a foreign object that has entered his body without permission. By doing so, this type of behavior will intensify the progress of the development of the disease, perhaps to the point of no return. Disliking and fearing the part of the body which houses the disease is likened to destroying your body while you are under the illusion that it is made up of parts or pieces. This response also reveals that you may not be willing to look at the cause that originated the disease. The fastest way to get rid of disease of any kind is to focus one's love toward that part of the body which holds the sickness. Let nothing stop you from doing so. By focusing attention and love, you will suffocate the element that is "diseasing" the body and cause it to go into remission, or alter the originating cause of the disease, thus eliminating any progression. The importance of focusing attention and love toward the affected part of the body cannot be overstated—hating or disliking any part of the body enhances the progression of disease because these emotions cause the bodily healing mechanisms to bypass the dysfunctional part in order to protect the rest of the body.

Acceptance of a disease is the surest and fastest way to heal dysfunction in the body. Unfortunately, it is a common practice to use surgery to remove diseased, dysfunctional parts. In doing so, the individual disregards the primary cause which underlies and created the disease in the first place—it becomes buried, irrelevant and unexplored. In this way, the individual does not need to confront himself or feel any responsibility for having created that particular dysfunction. In following social norms, it is easy to deny responsibility for the care of one's own body. In today's world, it is acceptable to delegate that particular responsibility to a representative of the medical community, and to put the well-being of the patient in his or her hands.

Love is not only an expression of feeling—it can be a functional attribute to behavior modification. Love is both instinctive and a learned experience.

One can distinguish different types of love and their connection to the overall response of the body, as love is received and manifested. There are different levels and depths of love. Love engages the recipient, and the recipient returns the giver of love with love. The result of all personal transformation work and the related processes leading to transformation are based on love. Love is a penetrating, gentle power, soft and intoxicating in all it's aspects.

In a personal relationship between a man and a woman, or any couple, who live as mortals, the perception of love is often the attribute used to disguise lesser emotions related to sexual needs and urges, jealousy, insecurity, and a predilection toward possessiveness/ownership. In a relationship that originates in a mortal realm, love often becomes a product of beliefs, myths and social conditioning. For example, the basis of marriage finds numerous reasons for a couple to join together, and often, the least of which, sadly, is true and unconditional love.

Love experienced as an immortal is not to be restricted because one may be "in love" with another. Certainly, one may love and marry a selected person. Nonetheless, a person still has the ability to love other men or women, and neither will take the place of the other. It is a mortal assumption that love is an either/or proposition. This is a self-limiting belief that severely diminishes one's options to love. Loving as an ageless being allows for so much more. The offer of love is one which can be spread throughout the world without limitation. One does not measure out love according to rate of return in the realm of immortality. Having enough love to go around for all others, without expectation of reciprocation is a key component, and a manifestation of self-love.

Generating love is normal and is an automatic function of the body-mind. The body-mind creates all types of love and levels of love to span the whole spectrum of being and the life circumstances in which humans find themselves.

> **LOVE**
> by Jennifer Perla, Winter 1994 & February 1996
>
> I love you because I love you
> because I love
> because love is who I am.
>
> I love you
> because you exist
> because you are a gift from the universe.
>
> I choose love. Love is a state of mind.
> It is a presence.
>
> Love cannot be given away, or taken away.
> Love is.
>
> And I love you because
> you are beautiful to me
> this is all.
>
> You can hurt me
> but you can't make me stop
> loving you
> or stop loving.
>
> I love you because I love
> because
> love is who I am
> and who I choose to be.
> I will always come back to love.

Volunteering your life

Preserving the existence of one's physical body is the utmost important function any human being can perform. Joining and being in the process of LAPI is to elevate your standing in the world to that of an observer of society, not one who gets involved in the mechanics of its manifestations. You can live your life in peace and in complete preservation on your path of life in complete fulfillment. You come first and there is nothing more important than who you are. You will do everything you can to preserve your safety and integrity at all costs. You will not volunteer or jeopardize your life in anyway, shape or form. When you are in the process and beyond, you will not volunteer for a task which may endanger your existence. Wars and fighting are for soldiers, believers and crusaders for a cause. Your life is more important than any community, national or cultural stand. In most cultures it is okay to believe in a dogma or faith that, typically, becomes more important and has greater magnitude than the believer himself. The idea/belief is propelled to be more valuable to defend than the body. In the last half of the last century, groups and societies have been, and still are, involved in using men and women for suicide-bombings and other types of sacrifices of their lives, for the belief in nationalism. People who commit suicide minimize their existence to the point where it means nothing. There is nothing more tragic than the belief being that it is for the greater good of society.

For example, a trained terrorist bombs a target and kills himself as part of the bombing. This person believes his trainer's ideas—that he is going to heaven for doing this good deed of advancing the cause of his belief. This suicidal person has been told that he will be going to heaven where the "real life" is waiting for him. He has been taught that existence in this world is temporary, at best, and the sooner he leaves, the sooner he'll start living. The welcoming party will be there to applaud him upon his death. In my opinion, the difference between this terrorist maniac who kills and destroys others and the mild-mannered priest or rabbi who is dumbing the life force of his flock is none. The clergy's belief system regarding the future and the terrorist are the same. Those who obey are going to heaven, and this is a life that is only a hallway for the next true life. They both believe they are here on earth for a temporary stay, and their mission is to survive until the time of their departure. The terrorist's decision is to go to heaven right away. The clergy are taking their time and marching themselves and others there slowly, as they enjoy teaching and conditioning their flock the concepts of misery and pain.

The lesson here is; don't volunteer your life to any person, place, thing, organization or cause outside yourself and your divine one within.

Selfishness & selfullness

The definition of selfishness within the standards of our culture of death, and from the point of view of physical immortality totally differ.

From the prevailing current cultures of the world, the standard for mortality is based on the individual taking responsibility for the culture and society first, and personal need comes second.

All cultures, societies and religions express a negative definition of selfishness as a form of control on the individual's right to define himself. There is a fear that if you take on caring for yourself first and attend to your needs before considering the cultural obligation at large, you may become an independent being operating outside the cultural structure, and therefore your actions are considered selfish. Consequently, this will go against the accepted rules, and you are running the risk of becoming a pariah or outcast by your peers.

Physical immortality is the ultimate in promoting self love. Loving and being in love with oneself is the distinction between considering your needs or the culture's needs. This is selfullness at it's best. In my world I consider my needs first and the culture's second. It is about cherishing the physical body, it is about taking control of body design on all levels, it is the ultimate power to choose for your own advantage and benefit. If I'm the sole owner and CEO of my body, then selfishness is the center of all life experiences, as is selfullness. Selfullness is confidence, trust, responsibility to oneself and contributing to one's level of life force. It is the stand to affirm sovereignty, to take full responsibility for one's actions and deeds, thus energetically distinguishing one from the herd. I have no apologies for being selfish and living my life. I have utmost respect for all humans and their choices in life. The above definition of selfishness/selfullness is not in any way contributing to judgment or dishonoring other individuals with differing beliefs and customs.

In the realm of LAPI, you live and practice sovereignty, learn the self preservation techniques and methods to keep your chosen/defined lifestyle on track and preserve the integrity of your uniqueness as long as you need to. At some point along the way on the path of transformation, crossing to other levels in consciousness, i.e. the fourth to fifth level, we may not have to be as obvious and tenacious in the above stands.

At times, I feel I am totally into selfishness, for my own protectionism and in order to solidify my own stand and life beliefs regarding living forever. I am proud to be selfish, keenly in love with myself, and my world. I deeply and completely accept and love myself no matter how I am viewed by others.

One important thing in life is to acquire self-respect. The only respect that really matters is the respect you extend to yourself. Without it, you will be an empty vessel. In my experience, I have learned that I cannot satisfy some individuals around me. My energy and my stands reflect confidence and directness. I look others directly in the eye, and listen. For some, this simple practice may bring out fear, envy, uneasiness, comprehensions, inadequacy in their life and resentment toward me for having endless possibilities. With this situation, I do not go into fear and protectionism or waste any energy on their reaction to me, or try to pacify their fears. I disregard it. My life does not depend upon anyone's approval or respect, and it is not my job to teach or change anyone living in cultural morality and skepticism.

It is important to make a real commitment to change yourself, and, by changing yourself, to change the world around you. In most cultures, organized religions believe, as do most metaphysicians, that an individual needs to forego his ego for the sake of progress, and sacrifice his life in order to promote social harmony.

In fact, many groups pride themselves on performing real or fictionalized "exorcisms" to get rid of their egos. In my eyes, this contradicts the belief in the unlimited possibility of life. The ego is one strong, defining entity that helps transform the old you, to the new, improved design of your choice for your immortal future. The ego takes on a new role and new job when helping to facilitate changes and restructuring the image you will enter into. Becoming a "selfish" person is not all bad, nor a negative trait. The word "ego" has been given a very negative meaning and has been used as a tool in the culture of death to restrain free-spirited individuals who feel they are special and unique, and who have a need to take care of themselves. Selfishness is recommended for the preservation of the self.

When in LAPI, a person becomes the caretaker and the caregiver for himself. Selfullness is an important step for the implementation and integration of the new beliefs and the physical changes that accrue in the body. Becoming a selfish person is a good thing. Selfishness becomes handy when the world around you ignores or shames your overtures. It is part of the wholeness process, when confidence levels increase and the world starts to look friendlier and more manageable. By taking care of yourself, you may elicit all kinds of responses and judgments about your behavior, your good looks and that you are "different" or "unique". When that happens, it is a good sign of your progress.

Present history
There are many groups that have some great ideas about physical immortality. Some are using the physical immortality issue/conversation for keeping their group together. Others are using the idea for financial advantages. Most of these groups use collective logics, while ignoring that their members are destroying their bodies (i.e., smoking, drinking, drugs, obesity, and all the mortal traits that one finds in any group). These individuals are led to believe that it is okay to do things as they have in the past, as long as they remain in the group and talk about the ideas—transformation remains only a mental idea. There is nothing emptier than people who believe in physical immortality, while aging and dying bodies reveal that they are kidding themselves into a state of illusion. I feel they would benefit greatly by adding to their agenda more substance and meat—to create and work with practices to achieve and produce practical and beneficial outcomes on a physical level.

Being in such a group is nice, but that does not make you physically immortal. There may be a lot of sincerity in their voices and in their commitment for their future life, but it requires more than that to create an ageless state of being. Nevertheless, these groups, by virtue of their existence and messages to the world, promote and enhance the possibility of physical immortality. I personally would like to thank the groups who have invited me to share and lecture on my format of beliefs and practices with them.

Others on the path
Leonard Orr is one very special person who has devoted many years of his life to opening up the world to the beliefs and practices of physical immortality. His writings are very inspiring and are directed toward the masses to enact a worldwide change of consciousness. I like the direct input and the simplicity in which he expresses himself in his writing. Orr's commitment and integrity to the transformation of mankind is the highest of all peaks.

Sondra Ray is also a very special person totally devoted to bringing love and harmony through the divine energies and her many books to the world. Sondra is a conglomeration of light and joy.

There are many individuals who have achieved higher levels of transformation, changing and moving toward the future with no limitation whatsoever. Some are moving through the centuries and between the continents. Some just change form and reappear in different bodies. There are a few who live in the United States. The European immortals are sometimes called "Initiates", a very appropriate description for being physically immortal. I personally like it.

In most cases, the individuals who are in the process for some time tend to keep their identity secret. Many need to change identification every so often to blend in with the crowd. My decision to go public with my life is to put the challenge out to all who are ready for change, and to enjoy the support as I create my new life. I have also been guided and told to do so. Writing is not my biggest strength, but the subject matter is my life. I feel that I have no say in this matter. It is something which I must do.

Everyday is the best day of my life, and the next one will be even better. As I learn and expand my humanity, it is not a chore—it is a privilege for me to serve others on this planet with the highest level of life appreciation.

The decision to live as physically immortal was the most important decision that I have ever made. Having been in the process, I have truly become and live my purpose in life. There is no higher satisfaction and feeling of enjoyment than to be a mature human being in this process. The strength and the inner power that one emulates in their environment invariably bring love, harmony and pleasure to all of the people around them. They are authentic. They are real.

Changing frequency

The following are pieces of a Ramtha teaching (1991), translated as clearly as possible, which I find eloquent and useful. I like the direct and genuine simplicity of the message.

"One must become self-aware, to understand the cosmology of self to access other dimensions. We operate in 4 dimensions at best. You must see the truth of your limitation to go on to other dimensions. You must first have the experience of the dimensional level you are on…You must have knowledge of this plane before you can supersede it…You cannot drag 90% negativity to another dimension… We can analogically wash negativity through focus.

We are filled with arrogance and personality…Thinking is pressing buttons and watching memory…Give up victim, tyrant, all of that garbage to have dimensional mind. Surrender to that which you cannot contemplate. You cannot fathom your God from theoretical memory. Becoming a creature of dimensions is the most natural act of consciousness and energy, but unnatural to humans because you are afraid to be something else than yourself. A multi-dimensional being is in control of all…You are here to become greater than your limitations…Consciousness and energy is the lord that impresses the brain to change the mind. Anything you take from memory and focus on analogically, you will manifest in time. To manifest in 5th dimension is not to think about it, but to be it…The ultimate paradise lies in a state of nothingness. The unity of God is in a no-time space. You must collapse present mind to get to multi-dimensional mind. Be everything but you.

A master is humble enough to become anything and everything. He contemplates endlessly until he knows. It consumes his thoughts… the deep thought, focused always…

The more limitations that you break down, the less needy and less fear you generate…It is imperative that one become self-aware of what they have been, but also what a vital tool the image is…"

The body electric

I like the simplicity and view writer Joel Goldsmith expresses in his work, "Realization of Oneness":

> "There is but one Power operating in this universe. It is not a power of accident, death, disease or sin. This Power is the same Power that causes the sun to rise and to set at its appointed time, and the tides to ebb and flow. The Power that is operating in this universe is the same power that is operating in my consciousness, and it operates as the law unto my Experience."
>
> "Every phase of discord that comes into any person's experience is a mesmeric influence from which he has not learned to protect himself."

This is a very simple way to put that all living organisms are energetically operated systems. Everything within our body is electrical in nature and the subtle energies that surround us and generate energy in the body are able to communicate back to the universe. Our body's primary and sole purpose is to create energy within our cells and then transmit that energy outward for the listening out there.

This is a basic fundamental fact—every cell in the entire body functions like a little battery and a capacitor, which produces electrical current and channels the energy through the energetic meridian systems to keep the flow of current and energy moving unimpeded. Whether you know it or not, that makes you an electrical marvel. Your bio-energetic system is very sophisticated. As of today, science is still debating this point.

In today's world our top scientists are still sifting through and trying to make sense of the chemical and biological aspects and composition of the body, which only represent one tenth of total body function. Unfortunately, science is stuck on the mineral/chemical measurements that they can reproduce in the lab. I see the body as a bag of skin full of water, with batteries and capacitors running electrical current up and down the body. This current can be tweaked and manipulated. Our skin bag of water has no solid shape and can be manipulated and changed at will.

Understanding this basic function of our body can open a new world of possibilities for outcomes and options when dealing with the bodies' multi-layered behavior. It can be lots of fun playing with shape-shifting into endless possibilities. In other words, using our brains' capacity to change our body in any way we like. Shape-shifting is not only an imagery and mental exercise—it can change physical form and can be done by all of us. Start looking at your limiting beliefs on the creation and design of your physical shape.

In the organizational function of our body's systems, all things start and end with an electrical impulse. Nothing is going to happen within the body on any level unless there is an electrical firing (electrical stimuli) at the beginning, closed with electrical signal at the end.

Energetic connection
Let's look at the nature of the energy that powers our life on earth. The main purpose of our body as a viable, functional being, is more than just a biological and chemical material—this only comprises of about

10-15% of the body's mass—the rest is water that is contained inside our skin—I like to call it a "skin bag". This water, the majority of the body's mass, is the main energy conduit and where most energy flow is conducted.

Our body of energy, or matrix, as I call it, serves the following purposes it:

- produces energy and uses it for its functional operation;
- sends and broadcasts outward, summaries of the state of the body, 24/7;
- receives feedback from the consciousness grid of information—or universal energy; and
- receives supplement for additional life force energies and becomes current with the universal pulse—cosmic supplementation.

If we want to be accurate when describing humanity in it's basic function, then we can look at the mechanism of energy production, storage centers, transmission and transfer of the low voltage current with precise quantities to the right part of the body for a desired function. Each of us has a sophisticated electrical grid, our own matrix of energy connecting all the parts of the body. Different cultures have described energy as: the breath of life, life-force, spirit, prana, chi, grace of the Holy Spirit, vitality.

In many cultures and religions you hear the statement, "we are all one". What does this really mean? Well, we are all connected to the same energy grid, or the mind of the universe or consciousness, which is the information grid—the all inclusive information highway. Because we are connected to the consciousness grid we exchange information constantly, 24/7, whether awake or asleep. This universal energy makes exchange with our personal grid and connects all personal (individual) grids and matrixes and all matter in the universe. We are realigned with current prevailing information all the time, anytime and in no-time.

Of all organisms, the human body is the most comprehensive and is a complex computerized device, an integrated and self-regulated energetic system. It is a refined, and in many aspects, unexplored, computerized-bioenergetic-chemical formation which is controlled by the brain (the operation center), the executor of all processing—a magnetic, electronic firing system, all with gravitational implications. This advanced machine can be adapted to all possible living conditions on earth or outside it's parameters, if given enough time and directed correctly. Never underestimate the body's ability to change, and adjust.

One of the ways of powering the human body, in addition to cosmic grid influence, is energy and substances created by the chemical and physical factory of the body, excretory and respiratory system. This powering system transforms energy directly into matter, to satisfy the entire body's needs.

Magnetism, which controls energy flow, plays a major role in our life, and is one of the most pervasive features of the Universe—it is in all that exists. It harmonizes, balances and associates with other magnetic fields. We, as bio-chemical beings, have different electromagnetic settings in different areas of the body. In reference to this, it is my understanding, that usage of magnets for healing purposes for prolonged periods of time may actually have a harmful effect. Our bodies have a natural magnetic spin, which maintains harmony within the different fields.

As I have mentioned throughout this book, everything that exists in our universe is based upon and operates within the information consciousness matrix. Regardless of our personal level of awareness, we are connected cosmically. Information directly affects all functions that our life is connected too, and that applies to all that exists in the universe.

Kiran Schmidt is a physicist who writes very eloquently on energy and information, and how they are intertwined and connected with each other. A body may become dysfunctional when one experiences any of these informational conditions: missing, confused, overwhelmed, disconnected, out of date, wrong timing, wrong form, or wrong kind. These informational states can result in many dysfunctions that seemingly have no apparent or clear cause. On the other hand, there is informational phenomena like: keeping trauma for a long time, instantaneous healing and healing at a distance. Information can be delivered and transported to us via: hypnosis, sungazing, open fire, immersion in water, walking barefoot on earth, radionics, homeopathy, all broadcast communications, prayer and meditation.

The bird people

Receiving cosmic information from the universe can come in the form of verbal, mental or physical responses, like a body release. This particular event and message I'll be telling you about came in the form of an "audio-visual" documentary, a story I saw in one of my mind monitors. At the time I was asking myself many questions about physical immortality, and trying to figure out the depth and validity of the culture of death. I wanted to know if this world, as we are living in it, is a real one or just a make-believe projection of our mind, totally based on our cultural beliefs, with commonality across societies and species.

I wanted to know if we are merely living in a world of smoke and mirrors. Just a part of the imagination, where we all operate with one basic collective consciousness, that feeds us all with the same information—shared and updated automatically, with collective stories in an ongoing fashion. Is the magnetic field of earth the one that causes us to receive information uniformly? Or is the magnetic field itself the delivery system of the collective consciousness?

At the time of this exploration, I had just finished writing the book *"Life Unlimited"* and I needed a definitive answer to the question about how deeply humanity is based on death. And if the death culture as I describe it is all there is, then, is there a place for physical immortality or living beings even when living among the dead? Another big question on my list was: will my writing depict correctly the path of an ageless living individual? Are there real qualified candidates to becoming ageless? The view I wanted more than ever was one from a divine perspective, a view from my God-Creator's point of view. A vision of his creation. I wanted to know his logic and the basic programming skills that he employs. If there is no limitation in God's design, then humans live in an expansive world and I am that I am on my own.

There were many questions waiting for answers. I focused my intention to receive explanations for my inquiries. I was ready. During a weekend journey with a group of friends, I came to receive the following audio-visual script. It all started when I changed form and my body dissolved into an energy pattern. I could observe myself and feel inside me, which gave me the ability to participate and observe simultaneously.

My journey started when I took off up toward the sky, I could see myself reaching earth boundaries and I felt my physical body was very heavy in it's human form. I needed to cross to the other side to explore and receive some answers. My body mass changed form to an energy pattern which allowed me to cross the grid to the other side. I was pure energy, I felt light, I felt free, without limitation, all was available to me. It was like crossing a mesh-like screen, which was the boundary to the outside world. I easily maneuvered between the columns of the grid seeing myself crossing to the other side with such ease, seeing how the energy pattern moved between the columns, as I have done before.
I could move and transport myself instantly to wherever I wanted to go. The place I flew to was an island, a very familiar island, a place which I seemed to know very well. I was familiar with all aspects of the land. This was the bird's island.

Everybody had a bird-like face with humanoid features. The noses were in the shape of a bird's beak. Each and every person on the island had his own unique human face with a unique bird beak. I knew these people and I was familiar with the roads and the hills and the entire island. This was a visit back to a place I seemed to know very well. When I landed on the island I was greeted by Kim (no relation to Kimberly!), who was my tour guide, and my companion to all of the places I visited on the island. She tried very hard to show me the benefit of liking the place so as to convince me to stay with her and the rest of the inhabitants. At the first place we went to visit, there was an old couple who knew me and welcomed me to their home. They looked like old farmers and they showed me their garden and corn field. I was asked to have dinner with them. I was baffled by their behavior—they told me that they had been waiting for me to come back for hundreds of years—they had kept everything intact for all this time, awaiting the time of my return. I was blown away by this. As I looked deeper through them I saw that beneath the clothing they wore, there was only a bird skeleton. They were pretending to be alive for all these years until I returned to acknowledge their existence and release them. They wore nice clothing that covered the skeleton very well—a very deceptive appearance.

They told me that I was one of them, that at one time I had lived on the island. From the way these people looked at me, it seemed that they all knew me personally. The old couple asked me to join them for dinner, but I excused myself, saying that I needed to visit many more friends on the island, but that I would join them at the opera house for the night show.

Kim was with me all along, trying very hard to make me feel comfortable, working hard to convince me to stay with her on the island. It became very personal. She stressed that our future was here, and that we both could have a happy time together living among these wonderful humans. She eluded to the fact that the people here were very down to earth, simple, and caring. She herself wore a nice long flowery dress that covered her dead skeleton very nicely.

The whole island was one dead place—nobody was alive. They were all pretending to be alive, and played as though they were living as normal beings—doing their chores and behaving as normal people. During the day I visited many homes and farms, only to find out that, for some reason, the whole place had belonged to me at one time. The inhabitants needed to get permission from me to move on.

Events in the opera building, an old, fancy and glamorous place, were the main events on the island. The place was full, totally packed. All were "dressed to kill", in their best suits—I could look through them, see beneath the clothing, see that they were all bird-like people and were essentially already dead. For the outside visitor, it was impossible to see beyond the appearance. The perfect group of people, having fun, many with binoculars and fancy glasses to watch the show below. I realized and evaluated the situation on the island.

Again, Kim kept herself close to me at all times, using her femininity, her nice fragrant perfume to get my attention. Everyone was pretending and working hard to impress me of their integrity and aliveness. There was lots of smiling going on among the opera goers, lots of nods and winks to each other. After the show I told Kim and the others that I must go back and thanked them all for waiting and commended them on the good job they had been doing all along.

By now I was very disgusted with the deception and the world of death they lived in. I could not understand why they had waited for me for so long. I took off the ground and flew above the island and looked down, realizing the entire population was not going to leave on their own, that they were planning to stay and pretend with each other. I had a thought that it might be a good thing to bomb and destroy the island so the inhabitants could complete their existence. Flying back up to the grid I changed again to energy format and crossed the grid back to the other side, back to the room were I was laying on a mattress inside a sleeping bag, touching and feeling my body to see if I was back to this existence.

There were two important things I got from this trip. One was the experience I had in changing my form to pure energy, the feeling of the change and the movement itself, crossing over to the other side. This is an experience I can duplicate again. Second, I liken the story to a metaphor for, and it gave me a clear view and first hand knowledge of, how the culture of death really operates, with self deception, pretending and the playing out of roles.

Chapter 15:

Energetic Balancing

Frequency of prayer
This chapter deals with a newly rediscovered method of energetic balancing—the ability to use frequencies of prayer as the most natural of all methods and systems for raising one's life-force and vitality levels. I am acquainted with a few individuals who have developed different software to duplicate the ideas of the ancient Tibetan prayer wheel. I work with the Quantum Prayer System, a newly designed software that works in conjunction with others' technologies. The prayers we use are from many groups and faiths in the world. There is no patent on prayers, they are non-denominational, and no group has a contract with the creator for designer prayers! Prayer is a primal habit that all humans practice when they feel stuck and have a dire need to create change in their lives. All societies on earth without exception, whether cultural or religious, make use of prayer to connect with the creator or God, to request a wish for a change of venue in their lives. Prayers are the requests and meditation messages are the answer from source. (See end of chapter for more on this.)

> prayer = symbols = a form of human communication =
> frequency = resonance = request = healing

All living organisms are energetically operated, being part of the consciousness grid that encompasses all that is in the universe.

Laws of creation; basic information—quantum world
A lecture given by Don Winter which I attended years ago was the most precise description of the universe that I have heard…this is my interpretation of his fundamental views: Mind energy and consciousness

are the only source of energy in the universe. We live in a world of no time, where all there is exists in the present. Mind is energy and is the primordial source of energy in the universe—everything that is derived from it is harmonically related and is vibratory. Vibration is a thought wave in the universe, it becomes a wave, and the wave becomes matter. Vibration is the basis of all energies, the zero point or the natural zone of the vibration is where God resides. It is the controlling place of the vibration and it is needed to create the whole. All laws in the universe are vibrationally based, the same as music, light, quantum and matter. And like music, all vibrations are related and can harmonize with each other.

Our world is a harmonic universe—there is no chaos, only our confusion and misunderstanding of what is. The universal forces are all natural and they can be expressive or contractive. There are always two sides to everything: on one side we have the mind = cause, and on the other side we have the matter = effect.

As humans living here on earth, we live through our thoughts—our entire life experience is based upon our thoughts and beliefs, and therefore, nobody can be a victim to anything outside of themselves. Everything that happens in our lives is our own creation including accidents and death. *No one can create or effect your reality, you are the only one, and you pick and make the choices in the following ways:*

- within your cultural beliefs;
- within your acquired understanding;
- on a basic default mode; and
- within your conscious choices.

Using our mind energy, we can have everything we want or that we believe can happen—imagine you are on a starship, playing inside a Holodeck.

Living in this divine cosmic consciousness, we are more than just these bodies of ours—we are pure consciousness operating in wholeness.

This is the only state that matters, there is no other state. You cannot separate your physical body from the energy that runs it—you must have a body with viable energy flow to maintain any connection to the divinity of the universe. A being cannot be fragmented and be in a state of wholeness.

Only our own limiting beliefs prevent us from using our own power. Living without limitation can be the norm in your life. A truly living man or woman must choose life to be "alive", every day—not making a choice or making life-defeating choices is like operating on a default mode and choosing death.

The Quantum Prayer System for energetic balancing
Everything on this planet is comprised of energy and information. Humans experience varying levels of physical, mental and spiritual health depending upon how energy flows within their system. When one maintains their bio-energy system in a flowing, open and balanced way, they will accordingly experience health and longevity.

Energetic balancing is a way to increase life-force (or chi) and correct imbalanced frequencies which impede healthy flow of energy and decrease life force. Research on biofeedback shows that stress creates energetic imbalances and obstructions, which can affect any system in the body-mind. One avenue of healing, therefore, can be through stress reduction—more specifically defined as balancing of energetic frequencies, or energetic balancing.

The Quantum Prayer System (QPS) for energetic balancing is one such modality. This advanced program comes from the quantum physics world—it uses advanced mathematical algorithms and computers to broadcast the healing frequencies of prayer and balancing information to it's participants continuously, 24/7. Since our bodies are always emitting electrical impulses, the program can mathematically communicate information to your consciousness in the same language which the body speaks.

We use information from you that is unique to you, to create an "energy signature" which establishes remote communication with you. The QPS sends corrective frequencies that attempt to eliminate stress potentials that can be present with certain imbalances. When inner stress is released, the individual's own natural healing abilities help improve harmonic resonance, resulting in increased physical mental and/or spiritual health. Participants frequently report significant decrease in physical discomfort and blockages and increase in flexibility, relaxation, physical and emotional well-being.

This energetic balancing system may be the most advanced of it's kind, working in the spiritual (sub-space) realms with the most effective subtle energy alignment, available in the world today. Something like a modern Tibetan prayer wheel, it generates and broadcasts millions of prayer frequencies directly to you. Included is a huge spectrum of balancing frequencies designed for optimum health and advancement in personal growth. It can affect the energy of the unconscious on all levels, in an attempt to create balance in the entire system, thereby making it possible for the body to heal itself.

Oftentimes, one will witness a retracing process where the layers of stress and imbalance are released—symptoms may arise in a clearing of old unwanted toxicity. This can be experienced as physical or emotional symptoms and can last for varying periods of time. For some the balancing takes place gradually over time and is quite subtle. Every experience is individual and unique, but the result can be greater well-being on all levels.

Ultimately, the purpose of the QPS is to establish harmonic resonance within the body, so the individual can experience the highest quality of vitality in body, mind and spirit. It is up to the individual to take a leap in consciousness to a higher level of understanding and awareness to utilize their own intrinsic healing power within. Caring responsibly for the physical body, through healthful lifestyle and cleansing is important and can only enhance the support of the Quantum Prayer System.

Chapter 15: Energetic Balancing

Healing prayer = symbols = energy

The benefits that healing prayer produce have been demonstrated for thousands of years. Our QPS makes use of the "frequency of prayer" for energetic balancing. Those frequencies have been shown to have an effect on many levels of consciousness and information usage in the body, thus bringing about physical, spiritual, emotional, and intellectual wholeness.

The Quantum Prayer System is designed to utilize the augmented power of prayer to broadcast subspace frequencies of cross-cultural prayer, energetic balancing and multi-dimensional healing to the participant. Just as we see positive and sometimes miraculous effects from human prayer, the QPS can be thought of as a magnified and amplified form of this generation of positive, healing frequencies. You become a conscious recipient of these frequencies by virtue of being a participant of the Quantum Prayer System, connected through the information grid via consciousness.

The QPS opens the doors to far greater states of love, peace, joy, health, wealth and happiness that have been shown to result from effective and focused prayer. Please note that the QPS is a spiritual modality operating in the realm of the etheric plane. This program does not provide subscribers with any form of medical treatment.

The QPS is set and operates at natural, biological levels. The interface is not always felt directly, but happens below conscious perception. Increase in positivity, well-being, memory, flexibility and emotional balance can be noticed. Some people are immediately aware of such changes, some conscious minds will struggle with natural intervention and they need time to feel the effects. The goal of the QPS is to promote self-healing, not instant perception of change. So be patient with yourself, allow love, and trust that you are the only healer that can heal you. Healing should take place softly, gently, and naturally with peace and tranquility. Let the healing proceed and do not try to force, hurry or suppress it. Acceptance of the reality at hand and creating lifestyle changes are often necessary.

"You are the ultimate healer for yourself and your own world. All healing is natural." (Mony Vital).

Your higher-self will choose exactly what to work on in the perfect order. From our own experience, we recommend that participants remain on the program for a minimum of 5 years for best results. Also, the lifetime program is much better and affordable way to go. Some will notice shifts in their energy levels in the first few weeks or even days on the QPS.

Healing happens from within, only by the individual. All the QPS can do is provide you with balancing to enhance and support your own capacity for health and healing. One may have greater results if she/he is open and receptive to the broadcast of information.

If you would like to experience greater health, creative consciousness and well-being, or if you assist others in their healing, you may want to look into the Quantum Prayer System. It may very well be the missing piece in your search for vitality, detoxification and well-being. We support individuals, families and pets—all living things!

The QPS requires very little investment for such a high-level and advanced program. Being on the QPS system does not interfere with any other type of healing modality you are engaged with. It can only enhance the result of your body's healing ability—it is not a replacement for any therapy or medical treatment.

As explained earlier, raising the Life Vitality Index (LVI) is the first and most important function you need to achieve in order to create change. Keeping yourself open to change is the key. For individuals that have a low LVI, it may take longer to see any detoxification. For individuals that have a very low LVI, this may be the only option that they have overall to begin healing themselves. Think of it as divine intervention, your personal angel is primed and waiting to serve you—your cosmic backup!

Chapter 15: Energetic Balancing

Detoxification

The QPS inherently promotes natural detoxification and cleansing in a natural, organic way, to clear imbalanced frequencies or energy blocks from your matrix.

Detoxification is a natural part of the healing process. Humans in this culture already have all possible energetic "imbalances" (issues) present in their terrain. The higher the life force, the less likelihood there is for any imbalance to occur. But the average person beginning this program will likely have issues that will emerge as their life force improves.

Use your own wisdom, knowledge, and love to heal yourself. Just watch, notice and be present. Remember, all devices and therapies are only tools for us to use, you are the ultimate healer, only you can heal yourself from the inside out. The QPS is available for anybody that is in need of a breakthrough regarding their well-being, especially when all prevailing therapy modalities have not worked successfully.

Our objective is to help participants maintain a high level of awareness and self-love. The Quantum Prayer System comes in answer to the souls' call for a pathway to inward to love. It is a tool for growth and enlightenment—it is the way of the universe.

Things you need to know about the Quantum Prayer System

Energetic balancing has long been proclaimed as an all natural, holistic healing modality. Essentially, the theory is based on one very basic principle of the science of physics. According to Einstein's physics, all of the "stuff" of the universe is energy, energy moving, or vibrating, at different frequencies. Quantum physics goes on to say that all that energy comes in small, discrete packages called quanta, and that each quanta has a unique frequency, and that further, those frequencies can be read and affected. Proponents of energetic balancing maintain that individual human and animal life forms have energetic frequencies, as distinct from one another as our fingerprints, which also may be determined and affected.

206   Ageless Living, Freedom From The Culture of Death

It doesn't matter where you are living or where you are at any given moment, the QPS interfaces with you through the function of your higher-self, using subtle energies and information to communicate with your consciousness. There is no time and no space with this technology, it is all inclusive.

For best results it is recommended that the entire family, including pets be on the QPS program together. Because, as a family unit, all members are sharing energies and frequencies with each other (energies are mingled together). One person's imbalances will affect others' energetic matrix and will impede other family members energy flow. The higher the life force & vitality level (LVI) gets, the more overall energy will be balanced and harmonically tuned.

I believe that we all have our own timeline for healing, and we cannot hurry it. It is influenced by the body's overall stress levels and your willingness to engage in lifestyle changes. You cannot be dependent on the QPS program! At all times your higher self accepts only what is needed for the highest good of the body. You cannot be overwhelmed by our broadcasting of prayer frequencies. This is all natural, and all healing is natural to the body. Staying on the program for many years gives one greater confidence and piece of mind, knowing you are being balanced energetically and prayed for 24/7.

Participating in the program includes automatic frequent daily scans of the body for negative energies: "evil" energy, negative vortex, decaying energy, accidental energy, EMF and cell phone (microwave) radiation, saboteur's energy and any negative controlling entity (mostly from family members). Participants may also send a photo of their face only, like a passport picture, which is used for hemispheric balancing—right and left energies of the brain hemispheres.

During your time with Energetic Balancing, every 4 months you will receive an energetic chart of indicators that shows your standing at that time. This chart is an evaluation of the top 8 indicators, whether imbalanced or not, that you resonate with the highest. It is a nice addition to your awareness of self, so you can create more well-being in your life.

Chapter 15: Energetic Balancing

As you already know from reading this book, you are the only one responsible for your well-being. The QPS is just an additional side play, contracting intentionality for a cosmic resource of information. Imagine, an angel helper hovering above 24/7. As Margot Anand calls it, "my backup plan".

It's important to know that indicators of imbalanced frequencies do not mean that you have symptoms or disfunctions, only your medical doctor can tell you that. The indicators only represent your body's response to the resonant frequencies.

The QPS is constantly being revised and updated, with new frequencies for balancing being integrated as we become aware of them. The prayers in the program do not carry any negative implication whatsoever and are totally based on requests for healing and well-being on all levels of life. All relate to universal harmony and divine intervention.

My children are on the QPS, as is all my family around the world. For myself, I like being on this program knowing I can use this form of natural balancing for my entire body. It is just another simple thing I do for myself. It is totally a plus-plus program.

To get more information, to view testimonials, and to apply, check out our website at **www.energeticbalancing.us**

Chapter 16:

The Dark Room

Dark room advantages
Why would one spend time in a dark room? The idea of a dark room is to more or less simulate the conditions of living deep in a cave in total darkness for a long period of time without food, where the main objective is meditation, inner revelation and transformation. The advantage of doing this type of workshop in a hospitable environment is that you can avoid snake and scorpion visitations, and control the building temperature for your convenience! It is in total darkness all the time. During the entire stay the group can share in receiving new programming for transforming old beliefs and concepts. The group dynamic plays an important role in achieving the right outcome and results.

Here are some of the many positive rewards one can get out of being in this type of dark room environment, including:

- setting your brain function anew;
- resetting buttons for the biological clocks;
- discovering and reconnecting with the inner self;
- working with and accessing the divine one within;
- obtaining easy access to removing locked and blocked trauma;
- body programming made simple;
- learning to accept and use pranic nutrition;
- experiencing what is a true well-being;
- loving and nurturing yourself (all of you), as an expression of oneness;

- seeing and choosing your next step;
- revealing the most important time of your life;
- learning to avoid the parameters of the culture of death you are living in;
- increasing DMT production—one of the main benefits that occur in the dark, produced by the activation of the pineal glands from which pinoline soma & DMT emerge;
- bringing possibility for you to see neutrino particles; and
- experiencing many more transformative markers from the workshop.

Dark room practitioners may experience that dreams and sleep become more lucid. A state of continuous consciousness arises in which there is no break in conscious awareness—meditation can continue during sleeping and non-sleeping hours.

Future workshop information:
Location: Southern California. Time: 11 days and 10 nights. 8 days in darkness with communal sleeping.

This workshop is very safe for the individual. There will be lots of silent time to go inward during the day and night. There will be activities during the day such as: breathing exercises, athletic exercise, sharing, meditations and clearing work. For information, check out our websites at **www.darkroomus.com** and **www.energeticbalancing.us** or call 1-888-225-7501

My dark room experience
Mony Vital, Ph.D.

I recently visited Thailand and participated in a dark room retreat there. The moment I heard of the event, I knew it was a must to experience—living in a dark room for about two weeks. The retreat was held at Master Mantak Chia's Tao Garden Center.

Chapter 16: The Dark Room

I'll share with you some of the obvious things that occurred to me living in the dark. Keep in mind, each participant had their own personal process and the level of transformation depended on individual vibratory amplitude and physical conditions.

The first practical task was to be able to live in the dark as I normally live in light—walking, looking for the water fountain, finding my mat in the gathering hall, going up and down the stairs at least six times a day to my room, shaving every third day, and very basic things, like finding the bathroom or the door to go out! For me this was not an easy thing to get used to. I learned fast how to prevent getting banged and bumped at any moment, at any turn, and at any time until the last moment while in the dark. Some got banged and had bleeding noses and bruises on different parts of the body. It was important to watch for collisions with fellow participants when I was in a hurry. It seemed that no matter where I turned there was a wall there. I learned to walk with my hands in front of my body, and used them as sensors and deflectors. I kept them stretched in different directions in order to soften the next impact. I am sure it was easier and simpler walking in the dark for others than it was for me.

The dark room experience is an experiment in one or more senses being inhibited and deprived—living days and nights with light totally blocked out, and optional ear plugs to bring outside noise to a halt. This created zero outside interference with the inner listening and feeling of the visceral mechanism of the body. Additionally, there was no food available at all for the entire time of the retreat. Water was available for the participant if they wanted to drink, for some juice was available too. With no solid food consumption and digestion, one unravels the deep-seated beliefs in the need for nutrition from food intake that we all have been programmed and conditioned with.

I spent somewhere from five to six hours per day exercising, doing every possible move and stretch using the elastic rubber bands that I brought with me, and one plastic ball for bouncing and back stretches.

Ageless Living, Freedom From The Culture of Death

On the third day in the dark room, things started to happen with my vision. An "imaging display" occurred inside my head in my mind. I'll attempt to describe it and share with you my experiences of this situation in very simple words. It seemed that I discovered two separate viewing monitors that operated in my head.

The monitors of the dark room

Monitor 1 was an automatic viewing of images in the form of an on-going video without an end, which was playing all the time on its own. It ran 24/7 for three day and nights. The images changed every one to six seconds.

Monitor 2 was activated when I thought of anything or touched something. It would bring an old image from storage in memory, displayed as a symbol of the thought or the touch. The duration of the thought was displayed for less than one second and would fade as soon as the thought was over. Touch images were also very brief in duration.

When active, Monitor 1 displayed the most beautifully colored 3D images from my life experiences and the Akashic Records (universal storage of memories and other dimensions). The images were very vivid and merged with each other. One image would fade and another one would emerge from it or just get highlighted and come into focus for a moment. The images themselves were very unique and ran in the same choreographed background for a series' of images and then would all change and have a new genre. It felt like an endless video that was pre-imposed on me and was playing all the time however my body was engaged.

During the imaging display, the images were present identically whether my eyes were open or closed. This meant that the images of this slide show were involuntary reactions and a response to some type of stimuli that I do not understand yet.

When the imaging display was on, I could talk and describe the images as they emerged from the fade state. During the time which I attempted to sleep, the images were still running as strong as usual. In order to sleep I had to ignore monitor 1 and see it as white noise to put me to sleep. Sleeping was very brief—possibly ten to thirty minutes at a time, whether during the day or night. On the second day of the imaging display, I was on edge, beginning to wonder if this situation would last for a long time, and if so, I wondered how I would develop a strategy so I could live with it and function in the world outside. Specifically, I was concerned about the possibility that my driving would be impaired and that giving lectures might be difficult.

That day during the morning group meeting I asked if anyone was familiar with this condition. I was happy to learn that this was a temporary condition and would last only three to four days. One of the local employees in the dark room, who has been living in the dark room for a few years, shared an exact experience as mine. I was the only one in my group to experience this. Now that I had no fear about the imaging display, I started to experiment with creating different situations and to play with them. I understood that when you are energetically vibrant and your life force is very high, the endocrine glands become more active and they go into a resetting mode, and that may be the cause for the imaging display (reset buttons pushed). My video ran out after three days and nights, the vivid color pictures turned to black and white images for one day and then disappeared into a dark image of the sky and occasional images of light flashing lighting my monitor from different directions and with different intensities. The flashlights were present in the monitor regardless if the eyes were open or closed. At times, these flashes of light gave me a sense of illusion that there was now light in the monitor and that I could see objects. I opened my eyes to check the surroundings, only to find out that I was still in the dark and that these lights were not the photonic lights that we are accustomed to seeing with. Also, at times there was a major flash of light, more like sunlight, that overwhelmed the entire monitor, made it a bright light, and looked like a New Years fireworks display, splashing down in the dark.

During the entire time of the image display, I realized that any sexual arousal would be difficult. Monitor 1 overwhelmed and imposed its images on any sexual imagery and fantasy that might have taken place.

Throughout the entire dark room stay, I was mentally, emotionally, physically and energetically engaged, totally in the moment with my body. I experimented with astral travel and bi-location. The retreat is a great time to shed old beliefs, conditioning, to do clearing of addictions and work on mapping the future. This can be so awakening for the body, mind and consciousness when using the divine power that is at our disposal (the Divine One Within).

Upon my return home, I realized that the workshop was a great catalyst for creating a new future full of possibilities for myself. Seeing things (such as time, space, energy, action, involvement, outcome, participation) in such a clear manner, was almost like the future talking to me directly and asking me to do or be certain things.

Chapter 17:

Cosmic Connection

Being in this world
When on the path, and with the intent toward becoming physically immortal, getting involved in politics or in policy-making is not recommended. It is not your job to change society or to attempt to do so. That job is designated for specific individuals who will be chosen and primed at the right time. They come from the mainstream society. The job must be designated—involvement can be unpleasant and harmful to your health if you are doing it on your own, with the probability of endangering your life. Your personal well-being is the most important aspect for you to maintain throughout your life. Do not take chances, your beliefs in physical immortality are totally foreign to virtually all people around you, the idea may cause organized groups you are involved with to reject and get rid of you, in similar fashion to the old witch-burning of puritan times. Immortals do not get involved in any type of politics or political agenda.

True, there is now more freedom of expression and tolerance for new ideas in most civilized places—however, there is not enough trust in the conservative right religious factions that are aiming to control human morality and conditions. Just to illustrate this, as recent as the beginning of this century, two Turkish initiates were killed when crossing their country's border.

Becoming linguistically inclined to be fluent in other languages is one of the things you may master in the future. Languages are important tools for blending in with your near environment for safety and seamlessly interacting in the dynamics of the society where you are.

Traveling and movement between continents is very common and appropriate to immortals. Changing address and location every fifty years is appropriate, as you may wish to look for new and safer locations. Of course, you can change your address anytime you wish to. You cannot stay in one location (state or country) for more than sixty years(can you say why not?). However, you can come back to that same location again in the next century with a new identification.

There is often communication and recognition between initiates. It is a very close-knit group who support each other when necessary. Intermingling and friendship through the centuries helps connect the initiates. And most communication can be done through remote-viewing and intuitive knowing.

For the new participant, who is moving into a realm of possibilities and entering the process during this era of technological advancement, the timing is perfect to learn to use many new tools to advance and enhance your life. Be an efficient user of technology for your own physical preservation. Assimilating knowledge of the emerging technological trends may be high on the list when considering future forms of communication—it is recommended without reservation.

Also, it is recommended that you be well versed in all new technical advancements in medicine as part of world knowledge, for information only. Knowledge of the world is the basis for being successful in the LAPI process and having fun in this wonderful world. Knowing your world is as important as knowing the traditional worlds, cultures and societies. Here, I want to emphasize the need for balance between the involvement in technology and simultaneously turning and tuning yourself to the source.

Remember that since you will live forever in LAPI, you will need to have an income all along. There is no limitation with regard to the type of work you do. Don't hurry—you will have the chance to change your profession as many times as needed or desired. Proficiency in different types of occupations will be a great resource for interacting with the community, creating the income that you need. You will make all the money that you need for living. Remember, you are not devoting your life for the sake of money and materialism. You will make more money than any person you know because you will be earning money for a longer period of time! The objective is to live well, be self-sufficient, and have all the money you need to be the best you can be.

Always go first class in your life—treat yourself in the best way you can, you deserve it. For the beginner, remember, keep your job for now, at least until you have moved well through the LAPI path. In this world, learning and living costs money. You need to keep this in mind. Become self-sufficient so that you may enjoy all the excitement of living in this culture. Participate and don't be a stranger in the community. You can help other humans in their worlds. Reach out because you can/want to help others to heal, not because you need to or are obligated to.

Ascension
Ascension is an outcome of wholeness. Describing ascension by itself as a goal can help one to see new possibilities for future operations of being human. For the ordinary person, ascension has the least importance as a practical achievement. The idea of ascension can be confusing to the reader regarding its meaning and the type of practice to follow for it's achievement.

Ascension is described by most cultures as a state of miraculous transformation to becoming pure energy. Some describe it as a vibration or energy frequency that is resonating with one's consciousness matrix which is cosmic in nature.

Being able to ascend, dematerialize and materialize at will reflects the individual's ability to harmonize resonant frequencies of the body with universal light. Being able to raise the vibratory frequency of the body to a level where the individual takes it through the light grid is only one option to bypassing physical death.

218   Ageless Living, Freedom From The Culture of Death

To talk about ascension and tell you that it is a simple thing to do, or create, when most people are deep in pain and living in the death culture, is absurd. It is not realistic and simply a nice conversation. Ascension is not a replacement for death, as it is presented. It is not a viable option for anyone who believes in death. Sometimes I am amazed at how much energy people waste on mental conversations that lead people to more confusion and has no merit or practicality to any one student, or the teacher who lives in even greater pain.

Ascension is for the person who is living in LAPI. I have not yet met any serious candidate or practitioner among all the living gurus or teachers who are relying on past traditions and old practices for ascension. Regardless of how many years they have been practicing their methods or techniques.

Participating in the world
An individual who works diligently to transform themself, to welcome the incredible wonder of LAPI, can reach the highest levels of human development and spirituality and still effectively blend into the flow of events and dramas that are unfolding in the world. After awhile in LAPI, an individual will be able to observe life events and interpret them in a new way, without relying on old understandings, especially death beliefs. At times, the individual will be exploring like a little child, seeing the world for the first time. Sadly, this sense of exploration is abandoned by most adults, and, along with it, its components of unchecked possibility, natural interest in all things, creativity, seeking, risking, fascination and wonder.

When in LAPI, one looks forward to the future, to a time when you master living with ease. You work toward accomplishing goals and exacting wishes for life with commitment to eternity. You will develop an ability to exercise a profound control of the world around you. When in LAPI, one masters the observation of situations unfolding around them, with the highest instinctive clarity a human can master. The advantage of a greater vision and a "bird's eye view", so to speak, allows perspective of the totality of events which occur in one's life, including the outcome of them. The ability of knowing outcomes will be a normal operation in one's life. Intuition, visions, and communication from beyond will become ordinary and a standard part of the human repertoire.

Transforming

In a physically immortal state of being, preserving and protecting your life in all of its facets, and helping in the lives of others are the most important virtues for you. Love of life and the world becomes the central focus in your life. The physical body contains all of you, including all your spirituality, all of your mind's greatness, and all of your energy. The physical body is pivotal and vitally important in this reality. This work is to elevate our consciousness to its highest level and to learn to operate in other dimensions.

In a mortal state of being, one lives in a very dense vibratory state. There is limitation in awareness that keeps the human being in a holding pattern and prevents the vision of unlimited possibility. For most mortals, it is not possible to operate in a dimension higher than the fourth, which is the realm of physicality and gravitational magnetism. It can be very scary for a person to shed all of the beliefs he or she has acquired throughout life. It is like emptying all the contents of your being, to become naked, vulnerable and formless, and then to wait for an infusion of love.

In many cases, this level of discomfort will cause a person to defend his old beliefs to a point where they become more important than his own physical being or any kind of change.

On a larger scale, transforming society will be a huge difficulty because the civilization is relying upon the practices of a culture of death as the basis for their identity, as well as the structure of it's groups and communities. With this kind of change, society as a whole will descend into a period of being in shambles and will deteriorate rapidly as their core beliefs collapse and their leaders are revealed as frauds. The world is presently under a thick cover of dark matter that prevents any advancement towards the light.

Ageless Living, Freedom From The Culture of Death

Earth's inhabitants are deeply enmeshed in the primitive beliefs that are roped around their necks. It may take years to penetrate this massive and thick shield that is like a shell around human consciousness.

In today's political environment, there is a backward movement toward bringing organized religion to policy-making. In today's U.S. state of the state, we are living in the greatest deception ever perpetrated on the naïve American public since it's creation. Looking from another perspective, I can see the highjacking of the U.S. Constitution and the termination of old held traditions of individual freedom and sovereignty.

A new possibility will be brought to the world, one individual at a time. A shift is on its way and will gain huge momentum during the next thirty years. There will be enough understanding and support to open up the doors to the entire inhabitancy of earth. This search for a new truth will bond the entire earth as one entity. It will prevail after the demise of the organized religions. God has never signed a contract nor leased any of his power to any one religious group. Movement into a new paradigm is not limited to any one group, religion or affiliation.

The most important work to be created by us, the immortals, is to prepare and transform life around us, to create the correct environment and facilitate this new awakening and new realization of what life is truly all about—joy and love.

Names for the living

There are many names from which to choose to describe a person truly mastering LAPI for some years. They include—adept, sage, master, initiate and others. Every culture or religion has its own specific name to identify this type of human. These terms attempt to describe the qualities, physical and mental attributes, identity and purpose of physical immortality. My favorite choice is one that is used in the Western culture—"initiate", a word with a multitude of meanings.

Cyril Scott, in his eloquent description in *"The Initiate"* (1920), captures the vision and the strength of the outside world-view of the initiate.

I highly recommended reading this book. I integrated some of his extraordinary vision into my life, and writing this book reflects the spirit of freedom and love I assimilated. Throughout, the practice of LAPI, even an ordinary person from the culture can notice certain characteristics of behavior which identify an initiate/immortal. This person stands out from the others, has a very healthy appearance, is vibrant, calm, self-assured, secure, and possesses an abundance of love and empathy towards all. An initiate may extend a deep, personal support, understanding, interest and concern for other individuals' lives as well as for the whole community.

The initiate will sometimes use imitation in order to blend with to society and its behaviors so that he will be able to mix in with common individuals and the environment. Initiates exist all over the world and live among us in every culture. For a person who wants to search to find one, it takes knowledge, resolve and specific beliefs to begin such a search. To be able to meet one, a person needs to have certain, specific knowledge of LAPI, or he himself has to be in the process. It is good to remember that like attracts like.

To see yourself as an initiate—imagine a vision of your "future-self", the ultimate person you may wish to become, regarding your essence, purpose, lifestyle and the entirety of who you are. The possibility of being the designer of the person you desire to be, starts first as a vision. Staying in LAPI can bring this vision to reality. Imagine a human being that has no flaws, weaknesses, drawbacks or limitations that are inherent in the tradition of the culture of ordinary individuals. This "future-self" practices unconditional love with all fellow humans, reflecting shine and emitting light in all directions in the form of warmth, affection, empathy, safety and knowledge. This light is the power that emanates from within the body, and it is this ability to display and transmit this specific energy of confidence and assurance about the state of his safety and his embrace of the universal laws that identifies an initiate.

LAPI is a commitment to create a positive outcome for yourself and in the lives of other humans. This is the highest purpose any individual can choose—devoting themself to and taking on the task of bringing awareness, clarity and possibilities to the lives of the innocent others.

The creator

In this culture and society, we call the creator "God", for lack of a better word. The term God isn't always an appropriate term to define the creative force. In the beliefs entertained by a death culture and who insist on only one God—even though God is written in the plural in the Old Testament the name of God is "Elohim", or many Gods, it is almost unacceptable for any organized religion to acknowledge the possibility of more than one God or a group of Gods working together. The creator or creative force is not an individual entity responsible for the entire universe. It is a force which resides within and is available to, each and every one of us. That unsettling idea can confuse and unravel the worshippers' old beliefs. Organized religions may lose their credibility in the eyes of their followers when this kind of idea is individually recognized.

One can communicate with their creator directly, truly bypassing the veil of cultural ignorance. God becomes a real creator in one's life, and the possibility to see, feel, touch, hear and communicate with Him allows for a new relationship and a new prospect of functional dependency.

From "Bloodline of the Holy Grail" by Sir Laurence Gardner

> "…To understand the root of the laws and customs which applied in the Gospel era, it is necessary to step back again in time to see how and why those laws were contrived. In doing this (with the aid of first-hand documentary evidence) we can see that so much of what became religious dogma was born out of fear—hence the expression "God fearing". In an attempt to forge a male dominated society from the time of Moses, such important figures as the once venerated wives of Jehovah were forsaken and this led to a loss of the earthly female ethic which caused no end in insurmountable problems for the generations to follow, even down to date."

I would expand on this idea to say that these roots led to a society of individuals who are controlled and suppressed by religion, where fear, death and oppression were and are the rule.

Conclusion

Hopefully this work has given you a starting point in the process of living as physically immortal. All of the processes, the personal and behavioral techniques, the methods and the experiences are presented to help you to begin a new life. It is not important what or where the starting point is for you, it can be at any place. Once you are committed to changing your old ways, you start a marvelous process that leads you to the flow of physical immortality. You need to be totally committed to your life, without wavering. You cannot live successfully in this world for any other reason other than to find the purpose of your existence and to improve the quality of your life.

You know by now that many people will shy away from this work because they consider the opinions of others more important than their lives. This response is just fine, not all people are at the same level of personal awakening. What are your choices? To choose life, and become healthy, happy, confident and in control of your future, without limitation. Or to choose death and continue your journey in misery lane with others, or at best, a life of mediocrity.

This transformational work is simply achievable, and can be supported with the outside work of specific therapies and educational practices. Therapeutic processes are available anywhere and are easily done with the help and direction of an expert clinician. You may need to search a little for an adept therapist. No need to despair if you do not reach all the marker points as quickly as your mind wants to. This process is the basis for becoming a truly "alive" human being. This level of transformation may be achieved by mastering all the pieces and putting them together. You will find that some parts of it can be more easily adapted and acquired than others. Think of this work as a manual that a person needs to be born with.

Ageless Living, Freedom From The Culture of Death

I like to say that patience is a virtue and procrastination is a flaw. The idea is to achieve all that you need to continue your evolution, no matter how long it takes. While doing so, you will experience a life full of enjoyment, fun, and above all, your health will be exceptionally promising. With every day that passes you will grow stronger and more confident about your future and your present. It is fun to observe your own moves and growth, knowing and appreciating the changes. Having a relationship with yourself becomes a journey of discovery. It is truly remarkable to experience a heightened awareness and the way it plays itself out.

We have been told that all humans have the same characteristics, and that there are common behaviors that put us all in the same group. Perhaps, but there are many differences among individuals. To start with, the biggest difference is in the level at which a person defines his or her own life—beliefs, conditioning and habits. In addition, we all have our own unique personal energetic frequency! At the same time, as part of the universe, we all connect in the field of a matrix of consciousness when communicating, sending and receiving energy and information.

The big factor is determining to what degree death beliefs have been implanted within you. There are two parts to the issue which you need to recognize. On the one hand, there is your individuality and the life impulses that remain in you, and on the other is the influence of the culture that has sadly penetrated your body-mind. Most people know the facts, and they are aware of the influence, but are coerced into the will of society. Many do not want to make waves, "rock the boat", question what is acceptable as the norm, or to do what it takes to change. One great challenge that you will need to cope with is standing in front of a mirror, looking at yourself and accepting what you see. The second challenge will be standing in front of your family and friends and keeping the personal integrity of your beliefs intact. They will view you as a lost soul or as a freakish, abnormal, aberrant and elitist who is riding another craze that will soon be passing.

Chapter 17: Cosmic Connection

I remember a time when someone in my life stood in front of me, staring at my body, and, in a calculated voice slowly told me that very soon another fad would be arriving that I would be telling him about. This person belittled my stand on physical immortality as a temporary experience that would fade away and asked loudly, "What will you do when this is over?" I viewed the facial expression as a wave of energy from the gloating judgment that reached my space and touched me. I was caught off guard, but in a very calm and comforting voice I responded, "it's okay for you to think like that, I have chosen to live forever".

Don't be surprised. People will react to your new beliefs with reservation, and sometimes they will ridicule your ideas as phony. Individuals who are experiencing major private difficulties or illnesses will likely see your lifestyle as a pretense or a cover-up of the real misery underneath. Their belief in the system is so strong that they must play the game all the way. Otherwise, the basis of their beliefs would collapse, lessening their social support. They would open their life to scrutiny by their own skeptical voices, questioning their core beliefs, which could lead them to a "near-death experience"—in that they would replay all the events of their life and find out that they really have no life period. They may then blame somebody else for the condition of their life and realize they have no power of their own, and hopelessness will be the theme in their "near future".

Some people will look at your beliefs and the practice of physical immortality as a suspect mental exercise to cover up pain and misery. This is a possibility only if you are limiting your new exploration to the mental acceptance of physical immortality, without addressing the actual physical body. I mean practicing only with your mind, while using up your energy without the abilities to regenerate your energetic resources (i.e., breath, programming, etc). As I discussed previously, this also occurs in many groups and associations who have organized around the concepts of physical immortality, rather than practicing the disciplines required for the body's well-being in real time practicality.

226   Ageless Living, Freedom From The Culture of Death

Love is the language of the immortals. To live as an immortal, an individual must understand that this is a commitment for life. A true commitment in all aspects of life—there is no partial stand to take, and a half-hearted commitment doesn't work. This is the most joyous way to live one's life, when the body-mind is working in unison in all aspects of life and operation.

By reading this book you are taking the first step to acquire a view of what your life is about, and to see whether you are ready for conscious change. It is all up to you, it has nothing to do with karmic imposition on your life. A choice must be made—you can go with life and play a "living video" in your mind, or choose death. You already have the death experiences intact to fall back on and what do you have to lose but your limitation.

I am happy to be born on this planet at this time, despite all of the apparent limitations. My greatest realization and passion is that there is nothing which any human cannot do and master. My experience in cultures where death is the most overwhelming factor, causing no end of suffering, has brought me to the place where I now make my residence, in a world where light, love and freedom reign. I want to thank you for reading this book and hope that the information I share can help usher you into a new reality. I am with you all the way!

Appendix

Mony Vital, PhD
PO Box 1070
Del Mar, CA 92014

1-888- 225-7501

1-800-701-9375

agelesslivingbook.com

energeticbalancing.us

prayerswithlove.com

physicalimmortality.net

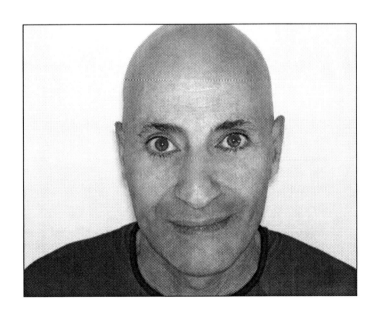

Naturalcures.com
energeticbalancing.com
Cyril Scott The initiate